MUSHROOMS

AND

MANKIND

The Impact of Mushrooms on
Human Consciousness and Religion

James Arthur

Published 2000
The Book Tree
Escondido, CA

MUSHROOMS AND MANKIND:
The Impact of Mushroom on Human Consciousness and Religion

ISBN 1-58509-151-0

©2000
JAMES ARTHUR

Cover image:

Special thanks to Paul Lindgren for the cover image. Jesus depicted as the Lord of magical plants at the Canterbury Psalter, Canterbury, England c. 1147 CE. The Canterbury Psalter, also known as the Eadwine Psalter, is an illustrated book of psalms made in Canterbury, England, dating from c.1147. It was made from the Utrecht Psalter (c.816-835) from Germany. Collectively, they are part of what are called the "Illustrated Manuscripts" of the Middle Ages. The image is only one panel of 12 images. The original, for some unknown reason, is currently at the Bibliotheque Nationale in Paris.

For additional information visit James Arthur's website at
www.jamesarthur.net

Layout and Design by Tédd St. Rain

Printed on Acid-Free Paper

Published by
The Book Tree
Post Office Box 724
Escondido, CA 92033

We provide fascinating and educational products to help awaken the public to new ideas and information that would not be available otherwise. We carry over 1100 Books, Booklets, Audio, Video, and other products on Alchemy, Alternative Medicine, Ancient America, Ancient Astronauts, Ancient Civilizations, Ancient Mysteries, Ancient Religion and Worship, Angels, Anthropology, Anti-Gravity, Archaeology, Area 51, Assyria, Astrology, Atlantis, Babylonia, Townsend Brown, Christianity, Cold Fusion, Colloidal Silver, Comparative Religions, Crop Circles, The Dead Sea Scrolls, Early History, Electromagnetics, Electro-Gravity, Egypt, Electromagnetic Smog, Michael Faraday, Fatima, The Fed, Fluoride, Free Energy, Freemasonry, Global Manipulation, The Gnostics, God, Gravity, The Great Pyramid, Gyroscopic Anti-Gravity, Healing Electromagnetics, Health Issues, Hinduism, HIV, Human Origins, Jehovah, Jesus, Jordan Maxwell, John Keely, Lemuria, Lost Cities, Lost Continents, Magick, Masonry, Mercury Poisoning, Metaphysics, Mythology, Occultism, Paganism, Pesticide Pollution, Personal Growth, The Philadelphia Experiment, Philosophy, Powerlines, Prophecy, Psychic Research, Pyramids, Rare Books, Religion, Religious Controversy, Roswell, Walter Russell, Scalar Waves, SDI, John Searle, Secret Societies, Sex Worship, Sitchin Studies, Smart Cards, Joseph Smith, Solar Power, Sovereignty, Space Travel, Spirituality, Stonehenge, Sumeria, Sun Myths, Symbolism, Tachyon Fields, Templars, Tesla, Theology, Time Travel, The Treasury, UFOs, Underground Bases, World Control, The World Grid, Zero Point Energy, and much more. Call **1 (800) 700-TREE** for our *FREE BOOK TREE CATALOG* or visit our website at www.thebooktree.com for more information.

CONTENTS

A BRIEF INTRODUCTION TO ETHNOMYCOLOGY

For many thousands of years on our planet, humanity has been involved in a symbiotic relationship with plants. Not only have plants supplied mankind with a never ending food-source, the necessary nourishment for our bodies and life itself, but they have also served us in another way: an extremely important and intricate one, yet an often overlooked one. I am referring to those plants which, traditionally, have been known to pharmacologically expand human consciousness into the mystical/spiritual states. The study of these plants is called "Entheobotany," or "Ethnobotany." A sub-field (of this study), known as "Ethnomycology" is specifically dedicated to mushrooms which have consciousness expanding qualities, and therefore deep roots imbedded in the religious traditions, writings and indigenous knowledge of mankind. The term, "Ethnomycology" was coined by its father, the late Gordon Wasson. This line of study is constantly expanding as more and more correlations come to light regarding the usage of mushrooms in a particular culture or religion.

This is discovery of the most magnificent degree. We have uncovered the natural link between man, consciousness, and God. This discovery may at first seem abstract, wishful thinking, or even impossible; yet as the evidence presented on these pages unfolds, you may find that its understanding does not require as much of a leap of faith as you might think. What is presented here is, to my thinking, as well as many others, the most significant discovery in the entire field of religious knowledge ever to happen in the history of mankind. And you are now a part of it! We should be jumping for joy and shouting from the housetops to the people of this planet to put their differences aside, and join in the commonality of the understanding that each and every one of us may now experience that which has been, until this time, hidden away in the recesses of our spiritual history. We may at last be actually ready to usher in the "golden age" of understanding, as the age of Aquarius dawns.

Sit back, relax, and enjoy as you enter the incredible world of Ethnomycology.

The experience attained by the Entheogenic [En(in)theo(God)gen(generation)] use of this mushroom is extremely valuable, yet the rules for experimentation of this type are unforgiving. NEVER eat ANY mush-

James Arthur in the courtyard of the temple of Horus in "Al Khemit" (Egypt), 1999. Behind the statue is the entrance to what is known as the Holy of Holies, wherein exists an energy-field that can be felt (remarkably) by everyone.

5

room, unless you are absolutely certain that it is the one you want. VERIFY its identification with an expert mycologist. This is not a recreational experience. The shamanic "DEATH (and REBIRTH) EXPERIENCE" is called that for a very good reason (it is what it is). When experimenting with entheogenic mushrooms, always have a few friends along (as monitors) in case you need to be assured that you are not dying. RESEARCH this before experimenting. Plan a full day for your experience. This is not a scheduled substance, responsible and careful use will keep it that way. BE SMART, ever onward. Most of all, JUST SAY KNOW.

James Arthur

Ethnomycologist, Author, Lecturer, Theological Researcher, Shaman, Teacher, Soul Healer.

Amanita muscaria: the Mushroom that Shaped Mankind

A typical RED variety of the *Amanita muscaria*, the single most written about and mystically symbolized mushroom throughout history. As you will see, this mushroom played a major role in the formulation of nearly every world religion and world mythology. It is the primary focus of this investigation.

The *Amanita muscaria* mushroom can be found at the roots of most of the religious writings our planet has to offer. Yet you will find within these pages very little in way of endorsement of any particular religion. However, please bear with me when I interject my own philosophical opinions. Remember, I admit openly that I certainly do not know everything. This book is the result of a serious study of the doctrinal/scriptural substance of each of

The *Amanita muscaria* has continually provided the world with powerful and mystical experiences.

the presented religions, and an exploration into the hidden symbology and meanings within them. Although the sacramental substance is unquestionably present, the religious organizations themselves have obscured the knowledge of it. That is, until the political nature at the roots of religion itself had been uncovered. So what is this sacramental substance? Today's religions do not answer this important question. They explain it away as purely symbolic, or of no importance. Religion has polluted itself by denying its own source, and by removing the individual's ability to experience the effects produced by the substance that imparts GNOSIS (the joining together of the consciousness with the consciousness of the Divine). By the removal of this key knowledge, religions themselves become corrupted and full of lies; especially when the systems inspired by Entheogens condemn their usage.

In today's society it has become taboo to present the expansion of consciousness by the use of any kinds of drugs/plants in a positive light. Such is the case when one discusses government or religion (or any other societal norm) in a negative light. While I have nothing positive to say about heroin, highly refined Coca (coke, crack), or amphetamines (crank), I feel that a blanket assessment of all drugs as being DIRTY is not only unfair, but a classic case of disinformation.

Drugs, in the psychedelic category, are commonly referred to these days (by those in the know) as "Entheogens," meaning simply, "the generation of God within," for the experiencer, "the realization of God within one's own consciousness."

The facts are that there are many plants that have been known to expand consciousness, increase awareness of self, and initiate one into the nature of spirituality. Thousands of Ph.D. professors all over the world (in fields such as botany, ethnobotany, entheobotany, archaeology, anthropology, philology, philosophy, psychology, as well as a plethora of other interrelated fields) have written thousands of books and papers on the investigation and study of psychedelic plants. These writings have dealt with the use of such substances by spiritual practitioners in most every religion formed on the planet. Most people are out of the loop in knowing about any of this. Hopefully this will change. Throughout history, each tribe/culture has looked for leadership and insight to the local Holy man, otherwise known as the

Shaman, Healer, Priest, Mage, Sage, Yogi, Magician. The insight these leaders possessed was largely due to their experience and understanding of pharmacopeia (use of plants) and the insight offered by the use of these things. "Pharmacopeia" is the root of our English "pharmacy," or "pharmacist," and has been also translated as "witchcraft." Different tribes and peoples used different Entheogens, largely determined by local availability. The social power, respect, reverence, and authority held by the "pharmacopeia-practicing" native shaman was/is a major problem for government and religion. It is the wanton jealousy for the power and control, held by these natives, which, in turn, inspired the campaign to demonize and dis-repute shamanism and pharmacopeia as something of the devil. The Spanish (Catholic) Inquisition and witch hunts (the murdering of over eight million people, tried as witches, and the stealing of their land and other properties done in the name of God by the Church-government up until the 19th century) were prime examples of this. Also related to this church jealousy and greed is the matter of an estimated twenty million indigenous Central Americans murdered (exterminated), bringing about the near extinction of the Aztec/Inca/Mayan peoples, AND the all-to-similar fate of indigenous North Americans ("American Indians"). The underlying agenda is the repression of the knowledge of Entheogenic plants which, if it succeeded, would insure the people's loyalty to established religion in all matters pertaining to God, primarily due to the inability of one experiencing God for oneself. Since government and religion are the controllers of the world, an independent Shaman/Priest/ Mage/Magician/ Prophet is a threat to their power.

The sacramental use of Entheogens has just recently developed an even worse reputation. This is largely due to the lumping together of any and all substances used by people (whether used for spiritual or recreation purposes) and then classifying them as "bad" (for you), "evil," "vile," and/or "dirty." This prohibition fuels the propaganda of the corrupt and oppressive (monetary based) war on drugs. In reality, despite the incredible amount of evidence that humanity's origins of spirituality are inseparably linked to entheogens, governmental prohibition continues to rob each individual of their human right to directly access and understand the nature of spirituality through the traditional and ancient means provided by mother earth.

People who follow the government's lead in this field, without researching the subject on an individual basis, are usually quick to jump to conclusions and condemn things they really know nothing about. Unfortunately, there are many people who have not researched this subject and believe that anything the government says must be true, yet they have absolutely no personal experience or real understanding about the subject other than the government/media-released propaganda and disinformation geared to create their agenda-based opinion; an opinion really based on ignorance.

The agenda of the propaganda-pushers is not only sad, but actually quite sickening because of the way it tends to lead the mindless masses of sheep down the road to foolishness, causing them to become the unknowing pushers of the very same oppressive disinformation and propaganda which imprisons them, whilst believing the whole time that they are being right, proper, clean purveyors of the truth. As you will see, this subject is absolutely a matter of religious practice, and as such, must be protected by Constitutional rights.

As Timothy Leary put it so well, "Psychedelics often produce psychotic and even violent behavior in those that have never used them."

The simple reality is that plant Entheogens are spiritual in nature.

I prefer "Just say KNOW" to the oppressive fascist propaganda "Just say no."

One more thing before we get going...

Its the use of heroin, crack, and crank that the government throws on the table to cause panic in the minds of people, that has allowed them to erode The

Constitution away into a now historical document, by passing unbelievable laws all under the guise of stopping the use of drugs and saving our precious children from the "vile drug-pusher," while all along it's been the OSS and then the CIA in bed with the Mafia and local government officials that bring the highly addictive drugs (Heroin/Crack), that destroy peoples lives, into the country, and then distribute them locally. If you don't think this could be true, visit my website (www.james-sarthur.net) and follow the link on The CIA/OSS and the "War on Drugs." There's also a number of good books and other research material available on the subject.

Perhaps our favorite free-thinkers and musicians, by taking certain plants and smoking certain herbs (also with a long religious history) should be praised for the insight and understanding they have received in life through these things, not be condemned and thought of as dirty for their use of the same. Of course, heroin is very dangerous and damaging, and I am not talking about that. Besides, it is the highly addictive properties of these drugs that are exactly what make the Mafia/CIA/Government wet their lips from excitement (due to huge profits involved), not caring what damage they do to people. Also the natural plant Entheogens are not a hot commodity for them, partly because they actually make you think, which is one of the things those agenda-driven, power & money-hungry monsters would prefer you didn't do.

With that said, lets get going...

Artwork as Revelator

Amanita muscaria is a "good luck charm," associated with the four-leafed-clover in artwork and traditional superstition. It is not restricted to pictorial art in obvious places. Mushroom-associated symbolism is found throughout religious artwork as well. Decoding these religious art symbols has always been a favorite past-time of mine; it seems when you start to look, there is mushroom imagery everywhere, especially when the artist is one of those "in the know," as revealed through their usage of these special symbols. For good reason, as the story unfolds you find that the depth of your understanding of religious art is directly associated with the depth of your understanding of the symbols.

The Little People

Often associated with gnomes, fairies, and "little people," the beauty of this mushroom makes it a favorite for artists. Certain artists also reveal deeper symbolic information. The mystical aspect is generally reserved for those that happen to be "in the know."

Artwork as revelator.

The little people.

The Hidden Meanings of Christmas

After studying the *Amanita muscaria* mushroom for some twenty years, I fell into the company of some very enthusiastic folks who insisted that I commit this study to writing. It is one thing to talk about the many various religious writings which I have been looking into, and found ample mushroom symbology to present a verbal case for ethnomycological reference, but another thing entirely to compile it into book form. For one thing, in order to present a full scope of significant inter-religious connections, one can jump verbally from one religious context to another, traversing a wide scope of references in several religions, weaving an overall scope of the similarities found in each. But in order to write a book on the subject, I found that separating the different religious references into their respective chapters was the best way to go. So I try to limit the temptation to jump from one religion to another, and keep it to a minimum.

Within the study of world religion one finds philosophical systems. These are the philosophies which the respective believer adopts as their understanding of life itself. Stateism must be considered a religion in its own right, as even those who profess no religious preference or belief adopt a philosophical view of reality based upon a state/culturally conditioned belief system. These belief systems are also based upon religious philosophy, which are brought into fruition through media and popular opinion. Were the many state and religious philosophies to be based upon truth and justice, the world would not have an incredulous history of bloodshed, wars, and oppression. Therefore, religions and state indoctrinated belief systems share commonality of basic philosophical principles, and all of them must be looked into with an objective point of view. This must be done in order to dispel falsehood. It is not difficult to see that the condition of life on our planet leaves much to be desired. Societal conditioning plays an important part in developing individual belief systems. In some ways this could be considered a good thing, but in other ways it may be intrinsically bad. The study of ethnomycology can not simply be the study of religion and its association with mushrooms *per-se,* because by its very nature it must examine the philosophical principles of the religions which have an ethnomycological connection. I need to explain this in order to set the stage for what is to come within these pages. This is not only an examination of ethno-mycological associations throughout history, but is also an examination of those religions which show evidence of having ethnomycological association, yet currently deny this association due to corruption of their root principles.

So this study will deal with ethnomycology as a base, but will also delve into psychology, ethnology, philology, anthropology, archaeology, sociology, art, history, religion, myth, culture, symbology, and philosophy.

I will begin this book with the study of Christmas and its associated symbols and icons because after studying most of the world's religions and their associated philosophies, I have found this to actually be a religion in its own right, and quite pure, philosophically.

What are the origins of the Christmas traditions? Most people never think to ask this question. Those that do, find a seemingly complete dogmatic system of explanation. Then, of course, one day there is that discovery that Santa Claus does not really exist. But, does he? Many things have been written in an attempt to trace the development of Christmas. You can find people who consider themselves experts in this field, and even books on this subject. I suppose you could call the field "Santa-ology," or perhaps even "Santa-ism." Yet, long lost, deeply underlying the realms of simple tradition, are very amazing symbolic connections and origins that are either long-forgotten or were/are intentionally overlooked. The basic philosophy behind Christmas is if you are good you will receive a present under the tree, and if you are bad then you receive no present. In some cultures those who are bad even receive punishment, delivered by various means and personages. This is a very simple philosophical system. Santa Claus is an all knowing icon who reads the hearts and intentions of everyone on the planet. Each child is told the story of the round-man (who wears red and white) and his associates – reindeer, little people, and Mrs. Claus. They are also told the story of a miraculous worldwide flight in a sleigh which results in presents being delivered under a tree. Yet when a child reaches the age of reasoning he is informed that this story is all a fabrication. This revelation is devastating upon the psyche of a young mind. It is also at this time that the child is often comforted and pacified from the shock by very strong reinforcement that the religious system which the parents or guardians profess is indeed factual. And an attempt is then made to incorporate the respective religious traditions into the holiday as the REAL meaning for the celebration.

However, there is an alternative to this cultural conditioning and shock-relief system of indoctrinations into the realities of life, which is based upon truth and is much more interesting than even the simple traditional understandings of Christmas themselves. The key to this alternative is encoded within the icons and symbols of Christmas. To know the meanings behind the symbologies, to which most people only attach dogmatic explanations, is to open the doorway to understanding the very roots of many other religions as well.

Several books have been written about the *Amanita muscaria* mushroom. This mushroom is found growing all over the world under pine (& other coniferous trees), birch, and sometimes oak. The pine tree is one of the well-known central relics of Christmas. Under this tree is where those who are deemed good find their reward in the form of a present. A big red and white rounded mushroom always grows under the very tree we are to look under on Christmas morning to find our gift. If we can find that under pine trees, then this present does indeed exist. If we can find that reindeer are thought to be able to fly for a very good reason, and we can show that traditionally they carry people spiritually through the air in a way that defies the laws of time, then the story would be true. And further, if we can show that the philosophical idiom "be good not bad" is really THE universal truth, would we have sufficient basis for discarding the established religious dogmas which traditionally replace the Christmas tale, and instead simply expand the story to reveal the more esoteric principles upon which it is based? Yes, absolutely!

It is my assertion that the traditional day of reckoning wherein it is revealed that Santa Claus is not real, reindeer do not fly, there is no present under the tree (unless placed there by a deceiver), is a disinformation campaign geared towards conditioning the young mind to be unable to accept the information which is presented herein. I also assert that the devastating blow of the destruction of a belief, and the associated reinforcement of "Christianity" (or other religious system) is psychologically designed to support the replacement information which is given as a comforting foundation during a time of shock and crisis, and is explained as something that will never be revealed as false (like Santa and all that fantasy).

It is also my conclusion that this event subliminally plays an important role for religious systems that wish to suppress the expansion of consciousness through fear of the unknown. The psyche is scarred deeply when it is forced to deal with realising that it has accepted a falsehood as truth. And when it deals with plants and things found under trees, subliminally, one armors oneself against these concepts. There develops an unconscious fear of falling into the same trap. Of course this is also pacified through replacing the meaning of things like the pine tree. Interestingly, in some traditions the PINEAL gland is thought to be the seat of the human soul. It is shaped exactly like a pinecone (hence the name pine-al). Apparently, it is also an autonomous part of the brain, resting in the dead center, not attached to any other part of the brain; sort of a floating pinecone in the center of the human brain. Perhaps we have a lot more in common with the pine tree than we thought. This gland, and its endogenous secretions, as well as other relevant implications, will be further discussed in a later section. But it is interesting to note that due to cultural phenomenon, the pineal gland atrophies during youth, which corresponds to this timely day of reckoning, and even begins to calcify during puberty. This atrophy/calcification causes a reduction of pineal endogenous secretions.

The Santa Claus and Christmas traditions of today have metamorphosed out of many older mythologies. The icons, symbols, and relics that have managed to survive from the "winter solstice" celebrations of old, have a commonality that deserves some reflection, study, and perhaps even some reverence. Understanding that these traditions are borrowed ones is central to getting at the heart of the true meaning of Christmas.

Santa as a Shaman

Today's Santa Claus is a metamorphosis of many older mythologies, including Thor or Donner (German) who wears red and rides in a "Golden Flying Chariot" pulled by two Goats (Cracker and Gnasher). In a sense, these goats were the ancestors to the now popular reindeer. What would the red and gold clad angel be doing with that nice basket? An Easter basket at Christmas is an interesting concept.

Christmas is commonly thought of as a

Santa as a shaman.

Christian holiday (the birth of Jesus). Many Christian beliefs and traditions were borrowed from more ancient religions and mythologies. This is well documented by authors such as Gerald Massey, Godfrey Higgins, Robert Graves, Kersey Graves, and many others. The virgin birth, the incarnation of God, the sacrament, Christmas, Easter, etc. have all been adopted/stolen by Christianity and used as its own.

It is well documented by fundamentalists (apologists) that the Christmas traditions are (with a derogatory overtone) pagan in origin.. This simply means that their origin comes from the traditions of the country-folk (pagan). By contrast, the pagan origins of most of the other attributes of Christianity are vigorously denied. It is also very easy to obscure, overlook, and discredit the Egyptian, Mithraic, Germanic, Norse, Celtic, Greek, Hindu, and Buddhist roots by lumping all non-Christian religions together and labeling them pagan. These are certainly not simple country-folk religions. So to just say Christmas has pagan roots, and not go further, is glossing over exactly what those roots are, and discrediting their study as worthless. Christmas Icons, traditions and stories have hidden meanings. Although not initially apparent, a more thorough investigation reveals far more symbolic content (which is decipherable) than originally suspected. At the roots of this symbolism research is information about the secrets of the mushroom regarding its habitats, forms, uses, preparations, and effects.

Shamen of Siberia and the Russian icon, St. Nicholas, both play parts in the tale of Christmas, providing clues as to where Christmas came from and why there are certain symbols associated with the holiday. It is these types of clues that will help (the questors) in the deciphering of the symbols. Siberian shamen used/use (despite governmental oppression) the *Amanita muscaria* as a religious sacrament. It is used for spiritual vision, out-of-body travel into the realms of the spirits, and as a plant-spirit guide in teaching and healing. The value of the inebriant is placed highly among the commodities of the native tribesmen, fetching reindeer pelts, meats, and all manner of tradable goods in payment and barter. It is interesting to note that if you aren't quick enough in the hunt, you will find only the mushroom stubs, the rest gleefully gobbled up by hungry reindeer.

The Christmas Ornament

One of the traditions, of ornamenting a tree, comes from the tradition of "The Paradise tree," a fir tree decorated with apples (representing the fruit of the "Tree of Knowledge" in the "Garden of Eden"). This "fruit" will be discussed later as the *Amanita*. During Germany's Middle Ages, a popular play, which was symbolic of the paradise story, was staged on December 24th (the religious feast day of Adam and Eve). Two more symbolic connections with the mushroom are the candles and cookies that were also hung on the tree (candles = Christ; cookies = wafers of the Christian sacrament). This ornament is of particular interest because of its association with the fruit of the tree of knowledge and the *Amanita muscaria*. This indicates that there have always been people "In the Know" from time to time. According to Apocryphal texts and other older ones, the "Fruit of the Tree of Life" and the more recently added "Fruit of the Tree Of Knowledge" were originally one and the same.

So why do people bring pine trees into their houses at the winter solstice, placing brightly colored (Red and White) packages under their boughs as gifts to show their love for each other and as representations of the love of God and the gift of his Sons life?

It is because underneath the pine bough is the exact location where one would find this "Most Sacred" substance, the *Amanita muscaria*, in the wild (in nature). These mushrooms grow in a symbiotic/mycorrhizal relationship with the pine tree, which means they always grow underneath it. The symbolic placing of gifts under the tree at Christmas is a sort of proxy, present-giving action, whereby the celebrants ritually mimic the work of God/Santa/Nature, by placing under the tree a GIFT (actually THE gift). Big clue here: Winter brings rain; rain brings mushrooms, IN the mountains, AT Christmas time, UNDER the pine trees. Then and there will you find that which unlocks the key mysteries of the Universe, through a multi-dimensionalizing of the consciousness in a way that no other known substance can. This Gnosis (joining together of your mind with the mind of the Universal Consciousness) is what the Sages, Mystics, Teachers, and Prophets were attempting to communicate through their rampant symbolism. (Had they not feared persecution, they may have spoken of it openly and directly.)

The Christmas Tree

All over the world, people bring coniferous trees into their houses and place brightly colored packages underneath them. In Nature, this is where you will find the *Amanita muscaria* (under coniferous trees). The actual mushroom "plant" is the underground "mycelium" or "mycorrhizae," which is directly attached to the tree roots; the mushroom itself is only the fruit-body of the mycelium. The mushroom is literally the fruit of the tree. They grow in a mycorrhizal (not parasitic) relationship with the tree. Many people follow the tradition/custom of bringing a tree into

The Christmas ornament.

the home and putting presents under it, yet have absolutely no idea why. Even people that think they know, usually have no knowledge of these mushroom connections. The true symbolic meaning transcends dogmatic etymological and historical evidence, by revealing itself in the totally obvious iconography and historically associated myths and traditions.

1) Saint Nicholas is the patron Saint of children in Siberia (Russia), a supplanter to the indigenous Shaman.

2) The *Amanita muscaria* mushrooms grow under the Christmas (coniferous) trees (birch also, but that's a different story).

3) The reindeer, native to Siberia, eat these mushrooms; hence the presumed flight.

4) Santa brings presents in his white bag/sack. Mushrooms are gathered in bags, and *Amanita muscaria* sprouts out of a white oval sack.

5) The mushrooms are red and white and grow under a green tree. Christmas colors are red, white, and green.

6) Typically, the red and white mushrooms are dried by stringing them on the hearth of the fireplace. Christmas stockings are red and white, hung in the same way, and shaped similarly.

7) The Virgin Birth is symbolic for the "seedless" growth/germination pattern of the mushroom. To the ancient mind, with no microscope to see the spores, it's appearance was thought to be miraculous.

8) The very name, "Christmas" is a holiday name composed of the words, "Christ" (meaning "one who is anointed with the Magical Substance") and "Mass" (a special religious service/ceremony of the sacramental ingestion of the Eucharist, the "Body of Christ"). In the Catholic tradition, this substance (body/soma) has been replaced by the doctrine of "Trans-substantiation," whereby in a magical ceremony the Priests claim the ability to transform a "cracker/round-wafer" into the literal "Body of Christ"; i.e., a substitute or placebo.

Good Ol' Saint Nicholas

Saint Nicholas, known as the "Patron Saint of Children" (among other things), is the most revered saint in Russia, second only to the apostles. He is the Russian Orthodox Church's supplanter to the native people's highly respected local Shaman. A Shaman is a holy man that is well acquainted with a form of spirituality that incorporates plant entheogens which facilitate the NDE (Near Death Experience), or "out of body" experience. Saint Nicholas may not have been a shaman, yet the symbolism on, and coloring of, his robes could lead to such speculation. The equilateral-circumscribed-cross is an ancient symbol for Christianity AND the Holy Grail, it is another very obvious mushroom symbol.

The ancient shamanic use of *Amanita muscaria* in Siberia is well documented. Despite governmental oppression against its use, there are still many who refuse to accept the authorized state religion, and continue the shamanic traditions in secret. Just as the Siberian shaman (commonly dressing in red

The Christmas tree.

Good ol' Saint Nicholas.

and white) would enter through the opening in the roof of a home where a ritual was to be done, Santa Claus also arrives on the roof and enters through the chimney. Just as the shamen would gather the mushrooms in bags which they would bring with them when performing a ceremony, Santa Claus also (on the Holy Day) brings presents in a bag. The Santa Claus we see today evolved from traditions developed in Germany. It is fairly common knowledge that the Weihnachtsmann (St. Nick) was an amalgamation of older Germanic/Norse gods such as Thor, Donner, Odin, and Wotan. What's missing here is just as Santa flies through the skies in his sleigh, Odin (as well as the rest) rode through the sky in his chariot, which is depicted in the stars by "The Big Dipper." The Big Dipper is the chariot of Odin & Wotan, Thor, King Arthur, and even Osiris (of Egypt). The chariot that circles the North Star in a 24 hour period is thus also known as the sleigh of Santa Claus because it circles his mythological home, the North Pole. It is no surprise that Nordic/Germanic gods have a connection to mushrooms in their mythology. As Thor throws his mushroom-shaped hammer to the ground, mighty thunder and cracks of lightning cause the real mushrooms to appear. As the horses who are pulling Odin through the sky in his chariot become over-exerted, their blood-mingled spit falls to the ground and causes the *Amanita* mushrooms to grow at those exact points. The Osiris mythology has even more to add to this. To the Egyptians; south was up (north). Osiris was the lord of the underworld, the south, (south = down) which is why he circles the sky in the furthest possible lower (southern) area. Not only did Osiris ride the sky in a chariot, but after his death Isis found that an evergreen (cedar) had grown overnight from a dead stump to full-sized, which was understood as a sign of Osiris' rebirth and immortality. Interestingly, the traditional birth of Osiris is the 25th of December. The 25th of December was also celebrated annually by putting presents around the cedar tree. This tradition is at least five thousand years old. The birth of Horus to the goddess-virgin-mother, Isis, is perhaps the eldest representation of the goddess/son mythology, yet it is impossible to know this, or the real age of the astrotheological-Virgo/virgin-giving-birth-to-the-child/god/star mythology for sure. However it is the oldest source I have found; it is VERY old.

Drying the mushrooms was/is a necessary procedure, typically accomplished by stringing them up (like popcorn) and hanging them above the hearth of the fireplace. Shamen and lay people alike would gather and dry them. They gather all they can since they are a valuable commodity. Reindeer (native to Siberia) are known to be quite fond of eating these mushrooms. The mythology of flying reindeer reflects the supposed pharmacological effects of such a meal.

It is important to point out that this Christmas/winter solstice celebration, with all its various counterparts, transcends the world's religions. The reason that this celebration is held all over the planet in various forms may have something to do with this other commonality at which we are looking; it is certainly entwined in the symbolism.

Here are some other countries'names for Santa Claus.

Australia	Santa Claus
British Isles	Father Christmas
China	Dun Che Lao Ren (dwyn-chuh-lau-oh-run)
Czechoslovakia	Svaty Mikalas
Denmark	Julemanden
France	Pere Noel or le petit Jsus
Germany	Saint Nicholas or Weihnachtsmann
Greece	Saint Nicholas or Santa Claus
Iceland	Jolasveinar,. Stekkjarstaur, Giljagaur, Stufur, Thvorusleikir, Pottaskefill, Askasleikir, Hurdarskellir, Skyrgamur, Bjugnakraekir, Gluggagaegir, Gattathefur, Ketkrokur, and Kertasnikir.
Italy	La Befana
Japan	Hoteiosho
Netherlands	Sinterklaas
Norway	Julenisse
Russia	Saint Nicholas
Scandinavia	Julenisse
Spain	Balthazar
Sweden	Tomte
Wales	Mari Ilwyd
United States	Santa Claus

This list is by no means complete; it was partially obtained from *The World Book Encyclopedia*.

A Sacred Meal Setting and Service

This place setting and service was contributed by a very good friend who has always been an inspiration to me. It is certainly a real fine example of what a truly enlightened Christmas meal is all about. You don't have to read very far into this symbolism to realize what the table is saying about dinner. The idea of a "Sacred Meal" is incorporated into many ancient traditions that also celebrated the birth of the God on December 25th. The sun, as it reaches the winter solstice, ends its course across the heavens and appears to stop for 3 days, then it begins anew its trek back across the heavens towards the Northern hemisphere. This 3 day "stoppage" was mythologized as the death of the Sun of God on the cross of the celestial 4 points. After the 3 day waiting period as it began another precession across

A sacred meal setting and service.

the sky, it was thought to return to life. Later mythologies transferred the death on the cross to a hanging on wood, and the 3 day death to the Son (Sun) being locked inside a tomb. The fact that the mushrooms must be dried before consumption is another euphemism of the god needing to die, or sacrifice himself, to save mankind through atonement (at-one-ment).

This is only the beginning; and but only a few of the associations between this mushroom and Christmas traditions; there are more. Here are some synonymous names and/or terminologies given to this mushroom throughout history, many of which we will be exploring further. In fact, there are so many that expounding upon them could take a lifetime, therefore, obviously, this list is not all-inclusive. The Egyptian term, "the God of a thousand names" begins to make sense as this research begins to encompass so many other traditions, mythologies, and religions.

1) SOMA (Hindu plant-god). Soma is also Greek for "body."

2) Amrita (Buddhist Magical Sacrament).

3) Ambrosia (Greek, "Food of the Gods").

4) The Holy Grail "Vessel containing the blood of the God." (Note the Grail-like shape of the upturned *muscaria* mushroom.)

5) Fruit of the Tree of Life: Fruit of the Tree = the mushroom; the main body (mycelium) growing underground in a Symbiotic relationship with the pine tree.

6) The Golden Fleece

7) The Fountain of Youth: Ponce de Leon is likely to have unknowingly kicked over the very thing for which he was searching; the red *muscaria* grows under the longleaf pine in northern Florida in December.

8) Haoma: Islamic Sacrament.

9) Manna: There are two kinds in the Bible; see John ch. 6 to 14. Manna means "mushroom."

10) Bread of Life: Yes, it's the "Loaf of Bliss."

11) Fountain of Living Waters: Its alive, 90% water, and shaped like a fountain.

12) Hidden Manna: See Rev. 2:17.

13) The Cosmic Egg: The Easter Egg (What are we really mimicking at Easter? The mushroom hunt, OF COURSE).

14) The Prima Materia/Philosopher's Stone: The secret substance of the Alchemists (Get Clark Heinrich's book *Strange Fruit* for this one; fascinating!).

15) Soma: The Hindu plant God and elixir of immortality.

16) The Flesh of the God: The mushroom is very flesh-like and is depicted so.

17) The Fruit of the Tree of Knowledge/Life.

18) The Flesh of Jesus, and other Gods [(Take and eat. This is my "body" (Greek, "SOMA")].

19) The Hammer of Thor: The shape is obvious. Thor throws his mushroom-shaped hammer to the ground in a bolt of lightning and a mighty thunderous CRACK. Lightning is the mythical creator of the mushroom.

20) The Small White Stone: The infant state of the mushroom resembles a small white stone.

21) The Elixir of Immortality: The churning-of-the-milky-ocean myth describes this in a phenomenal way.

22) The Feathered Serpent: From its first egg-state to its snake-looking second state, then shedding its universal veil (shedding its skin) and finally turning up its cap (gills resembling feathers). The feathered serpent is cosmopolitan in its symbology.

23) The Phoenix: From the ashes (spores) the egg appears. Then comes the upturned cap resembling a gold and red colored bird (the gills as feathers). Then the heat (sun) burns the mushroom and it dissolves, once again leaving only ashes (spores), and finally repeating the whole cycle.

24) Ankh: Waters and life, or the waters of life in Egypt.

25) Rudra: The Hindu red god of the forest.

26) Djed: The phallus or pillar of Osiris.

27) The One Eyed Howler: The round eye shape which represents the vision of the universe.

28) The Eye of Horus: (djed-eye) Sound familiar?

29) The World Tree: The mushroom is thought to be the creator of the world, in many cultures.

30) Celestial Food: The food of the Gods in the *Egyptian Book of the Dead*.

31) Aten: The Egyptian winged-disc.

32) Fly Agaric: Although "Fly" is commonly thought of in association with the "housefly, there is also evidence that it refers to the act of "flying," as in taking spiritual flight.

Many times these representations are used severally in one depiction.

The Holy Grail: Mushroom symbology in popular myth.
Note the similarities.

The Holy Grail: Mushroom Symbology in Popular Myth

Amanita muscaria, long associated with the "Flesh of the God" in religious sacraments, was and is the true Holy Grail. The Grail cup, holding the blood of the god, is an obvious analogy for the shape of the fully-grown specimen and its juices. Note the look of the fully grown specimen. The imagery of a cup or fountain are two of the more pronounced symbols used to keep the understanding of the true nature of the sacrament a secret from everyone but the "Elite." In its infant (button) state, the *muscaria* resembles a small white stone. The pulling of the sword from the stone (a symbol of wielding the power), is another Arthurian legend connecting the mushroom to the myth. The quest for the Grail itself is the quest for the knowledge of the mushroom. The Parcival myth depicts paths (traditions), which are to be explored (but not adhered to), in order to complete the quest. This quest is described in the myths as a journey into the forest (the world) and finding paths (systems) which one may follow, for a time, but ultimately one must blaze his/her own trail in order to truly reach the final goal, the Holy Grail (the discovery and usage of the mushroom).

The search for the Holy Grail is a mythology that has become, through adaptation, a part of the story of the Crucifixion. Some of the stories incorporate a cup which was used to catch some of the flowing blood of Jesus as he died on the cross. This cup, like many other relics, was thereby thought to possess magical powers. Historically, the mushroom has been the container for the juice of the "elixir of immortality," or the "blood of God," in many myths. The final shape of the *muscaria*, with its inverted cap, is most likely the reason that the cup/fountain/grail symbology is used in the stories. King Arthur, as a child, gained his rightful place as King by pulling the sword from the stone. This is symbolic for wielding the power of the mushroom. The stone is a metaphor for the mushroom, and pulling the sword from it is symbolic of being able to crack the code and possess the power of the magical plant. After Arthur took ill (in his later years) he was told that he must seek and find the Holy Grail to renew his strength and re-acquire his power.

Christianity: The Popular Western Religion

Christianity is a religion with a dubious history, yet many of the doctrines and stories are worthy of study. It is a religion which was created for political reasons. Constantine, The Emperor of Rome, knew one of the most basic tenets of government was the control of its people. The governmental control of people becomes much easier and effective when that government is able to also assume a "divine" authority. Although Rome holds no exclusive right to this idea, they certainly have etched their mark on history, enforcing their particular political machine. Christianity is the product of a governmental council acquiring and examining as many of the world's religious doctrines they could find; in order to create a "One World Religion." They took ideas and doctrine from Egyptology, Mithraism, Hinduism, Buddhism, the Torah of the Jews, and many others, picking the parts they wanted to include, altering them as they wished, discarding the parts they did not want included, and finally compiling their own plagiarized (and altered) writings to create the new Catholic (one from all) Bible. Since this was a plagiarized AND altered conglomeration of many older works, many symbolic tenets have managed to retain their original meanings.

The primary purpose of this investigation is to explain these hidden meanings in as simple a form as possible. Much linguistic evidence, thoroughly covered by John Allegro in *The Sacred Mushroom and the Cross*, clearly demonstrates that mushrooms played a huge role in the written word. I will try to shed light on the basic philosophical nature behind the religion by examining and explaining the hidden symbolism in the doctrines themselves, opening up a deeper (though simplified) meaning to the texts. Keep in mind the particular points I will deal with, for now, will be those which have survived the cutting-room-floor, and simply because these things are to be found within (the bible), should not imply that this compilation of altered works is, as a whole, something I consider to be a true religious document. Once you understand where to look, the ideas presented here will unlock the secret meanings of the book we know as the Bible. Then I will point out the same ideas and symbols, as they are found in the pre-Christian world, which gave birth to these myths, in an attempt to trace them to their oldest source.

Political and even fascist elements, in the Bible, will be explored later. These elements are the result of corruption of the original source-documents, as well as the re-incorporation of older patriarchal systems.

The Christian "Mannas" Revealed

John Marco Allegro, one of the world's leading philologists, put his neck on the line when he wrote his book, *The Sacred Mushroom And The Cross*, which made numerous connections from sacred doctrinal enigmas and sacraments to the *Amanita muscaria*. He fearlessly attempted to expose the reality of the mushroom symbolism throughout the Bible, Apocryphal writings, and The Dead Sea Scrolls. He was fully aware of the criticism his book would draw, yet as a true scholar, knowing the importance of the information, he put self aside for the good of all.

John Allegro linguistically linked the SOMA (Greek = Body), the manna (Sumerian = Mushroom), (of which there are two kinds), the names Jesus, James, and John, the fruit of the Tree of Knowledge, and the symbol of the cross, to the *Amanita muscaria*, by stating that all of these names and terms (and others) were synonyms and wordplay for the hidden identity of the mushroom. Needless to say, he had the religious scholars doing flips. The biblical apologists instantly jumped on the bandwagon of attempting to disprove anything he said. Although he did stretch the boundaries (at least twice) of some established scholarship, the proof is in the pudding (so to speak) and most of his associations are beyond repute. Besides, it is apparent to me that anyone who is afraid to challenge established authority and scholarship would not produce or expose most of the things which I find of value. Love him or hate him, he pioneered the field wherein most scholars and lay-people alike are afraid to even think about stepping in.

Even though it was the linguistic links that first brought this to light, it was the understanding of the symbolism that drove it home. Once you know where to look, and that was well revealed in the writings of Allegro, deciphering the mythologies unfolds into a whole new level of comprehension.

The manna the Israelites ate in the desert is presently defined as a question. It is not ordinary for a word describing bread to be thought of in this context. Manna is defined in this way: manna = "What is it?" A Biblical description of this mystical substance will toss the reader some clues.

1) Manna was a small round thing that appeared on the ground after the dew had fallen.

2) If it was left to the warmth of day it would breed worms and stink.

3) Manna was thought of as being produced miraculously (i.e., birth without seed). This is a perfect botanical description of a mushroom. Birth without seed (miraculous) is due to spores being microscopic and not visible to the naked eye.

The mannas are described in detail by Jesus in the book of John. In this story Jesus attempts to make clear; of manna, there are two different ones and/or kinds. He describes the manna that he is giving the disciples (last supper) as the manna that bestows immortality. His statement, unless you have eaten his flesh/body (soma/manna), and drink of his blood (soma juice), you have no life in you, takes on a whole new meaning in light of this discovery.

The manna is directly associated with the fruit of the Tree of Life in the 2nd chapter of the book of Revelation. It is the reward for those who overcome (the lies of the world). The "fruit of the tree," the "hidden manna" and the "small white stone" are spoken of separately, but in the same context. All of these are symbols for the *Amanita muscaria*.

The Fruit of the Tree

This 13th Century Fresco from France shows the *Amanita muscaria* as the "fruit" (of the Tree) of the "knowledge of good and evil." Adam and Eve had their eyes opened. The Gods looked down and said "Behold, they have become as one of us."

The fruit of the tree.

The knowledge of good and evil seems a strange thing to condemn someone for, unless the Gods wanted to dictate what was right and wrong, rather than have them know the difference for themselves. Imposing their will (and law) upon mankind is not so easy when people can think for themselves, especially if it

The Last Supper (The sacramental ingestion of the body of God).

becomes obvious that what you are being told is right and/or wrong in direct opposition to what actually seems to be good and bad (The BIG Knowledge).

What we have here may be the future as we were never to know it to be. The "Fruit of the Tree of Knowledge" is the same thing as the "Fruit of the Tree of Life." The fruit of the tree that is to come down out of heaven and line the streets in the city of the "New Jerusalem," the city of the new "Golden Age." The same, of which, when you partake of it, imparts direct communion with, and the direct knowledge of, God.

The cuneiform clay tablets of Mesopotamia (at least 4,000 BCE) tell the oldest known tales of Adam and Eve, in the Garden of Eden, eating of the fruit stories. But they tell a different tale than what is in the Bible of today. Zecharia Sitchin has been the foremost expert in the dispersion of what these tablets say. The gods came to our planet in space/time/dimension ships from another planet called Nibiru. Finding Neanderthal Man a bit primitive, they manipulated the DNA to produce the first *Homo sapiens*. In the stories, The Father God, "Anu," remained on Nibiru, while two Brothers, Ea and Enlil, were the stewards of the new colonization. Enlil wished to control the population, and Ea wanted to expand man's consciousness. The High Council, and Anu, leaned towards the Enlilian point of view. But Ea was determined to multi-dimensionalize (open/wake-up) the minds of his creations. This will be dealt with more fully in the section on Mesopotamia. But for now, suffice it to say that the earlier stories portray the eating of the fruit in a completely different light, in fact the whole concept is flipped one hundred and eighty degrees. What was originally a glorious and incredible story about the hope and potential of humanity has become a primary story of a horrible fall-from-grace, and even condemnation of the entire race.

The Last Supper (The Sacramental Ingestion of the Body of God)

The concept of the literal ingestion of the body of God is highly downplayed by religious scholars of today.

Many questions should be asked about this cosmopolitan idea of the "Sacramental Substance." Unfortunately, the religious experts shun the notion, insisting that the entire idea is nothing more than symbolic. A symbol points at something else, not usually at another symbology. The Catholic Church, in the early 1100's, decided to have the final word on this subject by establishing (under Emperor/Pope Innocent III) the "Doctrine of Trans-Substantiation." This is whereby, the Priests, by their assumed holy power, claim to be able to say some magical words and turn ordinary bread into the literal "Body of God." This event is one of the biggest evil deceptions of all time, an undermining of the basic esoteric aspects of the religion, and is, arguably, the most horrible and damning event to ever happen to Christendom, and as such the entire human race. Jesus clearly describes the manna that he calls his body in the book of John. He repeatedly described the "thing/manna" as a substance hidden from the world, but revealed it to his disciples. Understanding the last supper story becomes as simplistic as it gets, if you know how to decipher the event. Adamantly, Jesus says, "Take and eat, This is my Body." This is the TRANSFORMATIONAL and MAGNIFICENT event. By intentional misrepresentation (by self-appointed or politically correct AUTHORITIES) it has been stripped down to a rhetorical runaround and ridiculous dogmatic interpretation by enthusiastic religious stumbling-block throwers.

The Bible, as we have it today, should not be regarded as an historical document. This is not to say that it is not very interesting, but it must be read keeping in mind that it is a re-translation of a re-translation of a re-translation of an initially altered plagiarism. The book itself (viewed in light of the possibility of what could have been) is a complex document that must have required some pretty intelligent minds to conceive. It is this complexity which so overwhelms those of limited intellect that it convinces many that it could only have been written by the hand (or direct inspiration) of God. Yet the Bible pales drastically in comparison to the thou-

Manna was carried in the Ark of the Covenant.

sands of Hindu or Buddhist writings in complexity and substance. Most who read it never know this because they are instructed to steer clear of any other religious writings, lest they become deceived. Those who become "completely blown away" by the conceptualization of what it must have taken to write such a document, have never seen or attempted to really look at anything else similarly complex. Therefore, they have no point of reference other than their own intellect and the one book they believe to be the only true word of God. There is enough written there to speculate in awe, as to what those who wrote it were truly experiencing. Meaning; had we been there, at that time (6000 years ago), to read the original text (cuneiform), and were reading it in our own native language, AND had been partakers of the heavenly gift (the mushroom), it must have been an incredible thing indeed. It is important to note, just briefly, that the concepts and doctrines which specifically referred to reincarnation in Biblical texts were extricated from the cannon by ecumenical councils. This is another corruption which has obscured the understanding of life in general for all those believers who will never know that this happened.

"Manna" means "mushroom." However, if you reject the philological (linguistic) evidence proposed by Allegro and others, perhaps a simple read of the relevant scriptures will sway you towards the possibility, and perhaps you may also begin to understand how the mushroom, anthropomorphically, can become the body of the God.

> And when the dew that lay was gone up, behold, upon the face of the wilderness there lay a small round thing, as small as the hoar frost on the ground.
>
> Exodus 16-14
>
> And Moses said, let no man leave of it till morning.
>
> Exodus 16-19
>
> Notwithstanding they hearkened not unto Moses; but some of them left of it till the morning, and it bred worms, and stank: and Moses was wroth with them.
>
> Exodus 16-20

Mushrooms grow from moisture, such it is that they grow after the dew falls. They appear miraculously because they grow from spores (which are microscopic) and have no seed. In fact, they seem to disappear as mysteriously as they appeared, leaving no visible trace. Mushrooms, as any mycologist can tell you, left in the sun, or otherwise left to their natural process, begin to rot, breed worms, and also begin to stink. Manna means "mushroom" philologically, linguistically, and, as you can see, mushrooms physically fit the description given of the substance in these texts.

Manna in the Ark of the Covenant

Moses built this elaborate device to carry the manna through the wilderness. To look inside the ark was punishable by death. The box itself is of little import, or spiritual value. What IS important, is what was INSIDE the ark. The long and tedious search for this artifact shows either a complete missing-of-the-point, or a deliberate mis-direction of attention.

There are TWO mannas, the one the Israelites ate in the desert, and the "hidden manna."

To know about the mushroom is to have the key to unlock the doors of scriptural interpretation. An "opening of the seals of the book" could be another way of looking at it. Without the understanding of the hidden meanings behind the symbolism, the texts lose their full significance. For instance, reading in the Book of St. John, connect the dots and see what it seems to say (with this in mind). Biblical scholars know that reading the reference (center) column, between the columns of scripture, reveals hidden connections between symbols and clarifies their meaning. I will follow these references to help guide the context of this exploration.

> Jesus saith unto him, I am the way, the truth, and the life: no man cometh unto the father but by me.
>
> John 14-6
>
> I am the door: by me if any man enter in, he shall be saved, and shall go in and out, and find pasture.
>
> John 10-9
>
> And wither I go ye know, and the way ye know.
>
> John 14-4
>
> And I will pray the father, and he shall give you another comforter, that he may abide with you forever; Even the spirit of truth; whom the world cannot receive, because it seeth him not, neither knoweth him: but ye know him; for he dwelleth with you; and shall be in you.
>
> John 14-16
>
> But the anointing which ye have received of him abideth in you, and ye need not that any man teach you; but as the same anointing teacheth you of all things, and is truth, and is no lie, and even as it hath taught you, ye shall abide in it.
>
> John 2-27

There are many layers of interpretation of scripture, and those that have special understanding get into the deeper meanings. This particular text may first be understood by thinking about what has been said at the surface level, and then looking for connections to the mushroom proposal. There is no way to go to the Father but by him, the door, through which you can go in and out. He will not stay on earth, but leaves behind a comforter, that will dwell among us, and be in us. If something is dwelling with you, and can be in you, you must be eating it. It is the door, the comforter, and will be in you. Going in and out means after ingesting you multidimensionally go into the spiritual realm. It will teach you all things. This is a description of the substance that you eat, which opens the doorway to the place where you are taught all things.

Understanding this interpretation of deep level symbolism opens up whole new vistas and possibilities for the individual. Perhaps the direct communion with God, sometimes referred to as Gnosis, is not an impossibility if one can get past the alien and unfamiliar concept of the mechanics of it. It must be considered that there may be a deeper level to communion than that communication or dialogue which people can perceive of (or imagine) within their own minds. This is telling us that there IS something here that IS available to us right now. Understood at the surface level, this just points at something in the future that (hopefully) is to be revealed. If the conditioning can be broken and the realization of this hidden thing achieved, then glory to we upon the earth because the time is at hand. Otherwise, it is simply obscured in apologetic runaround by supposed authorities who frantically try to explain why it is not this literal and obvious "THING." This also describes an ANOINTING (Greek = Chrisma, once again close to Christmas). We go right back again to the special holy substance endowing one with the gift of the holy spirit, the door, the comforter, which will dwell with you, and will be in you. The comforter (it says) the world does not see, or know, but those specially gifted (whom Jesus is speaking to) know, and see, and will have it inside of them. The manna, the door, the comforter, will teach those who know. Even to the point that they have no need to be taught by anyone. And this, of course, would mean that there is no need for the intercessory function of a priest.

Here again we see that those who know have no need for a church, pastor, prophet, or authority figure here on earth as they have direct communion. Consider the manna (bread) that comes down from heaven, and see if it becomes a little more clear. Especially in regards to this being a synonymous (one and the same) substance that is inside of you. This part expressly states that you should take and eat.

> Labour not for the meat which perisheth, but for that meat which endureth unto everlasting life, which the son of man shall give unto you; for him hath God the father sealed.
>
> John 6-27

> Our fathers did eat manna in the desert; as it is written, He gave them bread from heaven to eat.
>
> John 6-31

> Then Jesus said unto them, verily verily I say unto you, Moses gave you not that bread from heaven; but my father giveth you the true bread from heaven.
>
> John 6-32

> Then said they unto him, Lord, evermore give us this bread.
>
> John 6-34

> And Jesus said unto them, I am the bread of life.
>
> John 6-35

> The Jews then murmured at him, because he said, I am the bread that came down from heaven.
>
> John 6-41

> Jesus therefore answered and said unto them, Murmur not among yourselves.
>
> John 6-43

> I am that bread of life.
>
> John 6-48

> He that eateth my flesh, and drinketh my blood, dwelleth in me, and I in him.
>
> John 6-56

He that believeth on me, as the scripture has said, out of his belly shall flow rivers of living water.

John 7-38

The rivers of living water that will flow out of the bellies of those that eat the manna will be discussed later in the next section. Prepare yourselves for the task of breaking the taboos and conditioning that bind you. The meat, the manna, the door, the comforter, the bread, the living waters, the blood, are all synonymous for that which will dwell with you, and you will put "in" you, which will teach you all things through direct communion. For those who ascribe to the "OFFICIAL" accepted explanation, namely that Jesus alone is the substance, and that everything else is merely symbolic for him, in the next part we will explore the book of Revelation, where (as in John) it says that the world does not see, because it does not know, as opposed to those who know, and see, and will have it in them. Something that the world does not know, because it does not see, is certainly "hidden" as in the "hidden manna."

He that hath an ear, let him hear what the Spirit saith unto the Churches; to him that overcometh will I give to eat of the tree of life, which is in the midst of the paradise of God.

Rev 2-7

He that hath an ear, let him hear what the Spirit saith unto the Churches; to him that overcometh will I give to eat of the hidden manna, and will give him a white stone, and in the stone a new name written, which no man knoweth saving he that receiveth it.

Rev 2-17

Manna, as it has already been expressed, in ancient tongue (which this was translated from) means mushroom. It has also been explained that the mushroom is the fruit of the tree of life. In the next chapter it will be shown that the mushroom is also referred to as a small white stone. The mushroom, the manna, the white stone, the comforter, the door which you will have in you, which you can enter in and out of, which will show you all things.

What doth it profit, my bretheren, though a man say he have faith, and have not works? Can faith save him?

James 2-14

If a brother or sister be naked, and destitute of daily food,

James 2-15

And one of you say unto them, Depart in peace, be ye warmed and filled; notwithstanding ye give them not those things which are needful to the body; What doth it profit?

James 2-16

The things which are needful to the body, if we follow the thread of this discourse, are that which will be in you. The door, comforter, manna, blood, bread, stone, works (being tangible). It can be argued that all is well and that the body needs nothing, yet there seems to be direct discrepancy to this supposition.

Then Jesus said unto them, Verily verily I say unto you, Except ye eat the flesh of the son of man, and drink his blood, ye have no life in you.

John 6-53

Whoso eateth my flesh, and drinketh my blood, hath eternal life; and I will raise him up at the last day.

John 6-54

For my flesh is meat indeed, and my blood is drink indeed.

John 6-55

He that eateth my flesh, and drinketh my blood, dwelleth in me, and I in him.

John 6-56

This is saying pretty clearly that the eating and drinking is physical. My body is flesh indeed, and my blood is drink indeed, and the added statement that when you eat, it is inside of you, leaves little room for debate that this is a substance, not a phantom symbol alone. For those who choose to debate this I ask that they show me their "substance," because according to Jesus' words, unless you eat and drink of "IT," you have no life in you. By the way, do I really need to mention that this is not some strange reference to Cannibalism? I sure hope not, if you still think this, read on. Somewhere, some of this MUST convince you that he is not saying to take a bite out of his arm, or any other piece of his actual anatomy.

The Fountain of Living Waters

The God of the Bible says "I am the Fountain Of Living Waters." If we are to understand this statement on a level of literal translation, then this means being alive, made of water, and in the similitude of a fountain. This describes a mushroom. The "waters of life" is an ancient term linked to the living waters, and the "waters of immortality." These are the waters one drinks to receive the gift of immortality and transcendence. Soma, and Amrta (Hindu/Buddhist), are also considered the waters of life, the attributes of which bestowed enlightenment. The churning-of-the-milky-ocean is to (metaphorically) produce this substance. The waters of life are also synonymous with the blood of the god in the sacramental analysis.

Jesus was the revealer of the "fountain of living waters," as in Rev. 21-6: *he will give those who are athirst the living waters.*

Living waters, blood, manna, flesh, and all this "stuff" is one and same thing, represented in different ways. All represent eating and drinking of a phenomenal substance that produces multidimensionality (door), great spiritual learning, and communion, with God being inside of you. While the popular bread (or cracker) and water (or wine) do go inside the body, they certainly lack the substantive qualities which the action of ingesting is supposed to induce. In my opinion, the magical act of "trans-substantiation" has no merit. The statement of Jesus, "Unless you eat

The fountain of living waters.

Jesus with a mushroom cap, or aura?.

and drink you have no life in you" would seem to condemn the replacement of whatever the real thing is with a placebo (substitute).

> Hath a nation changed their gods, which are yet no gods? But my people have changed their glory for that which doth not profit.
>
> Jeremiah 3-11
>
> Be ye astonished, Oh ye heavens, at this, and be horribly afraid, be ye very desolate, saith the Lord.
>
> Jeremiah 3-12
>
> For my people have committed two evils; they have forsaken me the fountain of living waters, and hewed them out cisterns, broken cisterns, that can hold no water.
>
> Jeremiah 3-13

Being astonished at this is only the beginning, being horribly afraid and desolate is what is instructed. Being desolate certainly describes the author's understanding of being cut off from the presence of the Lord (true communion). But how can his people be cut off from the Lord? The answer is apparent in this section. It is because the true fountain of living waters has been forsaken, replaced by cisterns that do not profit (substitute/placebo), and are broken. If a light bulb does not work, it is broken. If an eaten substance that is supposed to produce the described results does not produce these results, then it is broken and (mystical illusions, or delusions, aside) actually worthless.

Jesus with a Mushroom Cap, or Aura?

A common depiction of enlightenment is this mushroom behind the head of one who is a knower, often thought to be some type of glowing aura. This may be symbolic for the spiritual glow one has after the change that is experienced by the heavenly gift of the Holy Ghost. Many artworks show the difference between those who have "tasted of the heavenly Gift" and those who have not. This is depicted by whether one has this glow or not.

I bring this line of thinking up because it has been lingering in the back of my mind for many years. Perhaps there is a loss in translation that would make this less dire. But if we are to understand this literally, it is saying that something happens to you when you eat this. Perhaps a spiritual change that somehow saves one from the second death. This has always made me wonder just how important it really is for people to eat this. You can see how, once the suspension of disbelief has been achieved, there is

Jesus in a "tub" of transfiguration.

a very deep desire to share this information with others. Much in the same manner that a fundamentalist Christian feels a need to save the rest of the world from hell by delivering the message of their God to those in danger of death by disbelief. The difference being, the substance that established religion is feeding their flock does not profit them. Simple bread, even after magical supposed transformation, simply does not produce the effects that are really being prescribed by these texts. This just makes it seem all that much more important. And it also brings into question the idea that those who convince themselves that they truly feel something after eating the priest-blessed bread and water, or whatever, may be creating an illusion that is eventually (although they think it wonderful) something that is damaging to them beyond comprehension.

The search for a similar sense of imperative in the other religions has not produced this same urgent warning. In fact, the time in my life that I have spent discussing the mushroom theory with many, many people, has turned up many other interesting possibilities.

Of course I try not to just run up to people and say "Hello there, eat this mushroom because I may never see you again, and it is very important." Although sometimes I feel like it. Mostly, it is a deep sense of love that I feel often (even for strangers) which causes me to eventually bring this subject up. There seems to be (as in any other field) different levels of understanding throughout the world regarding the mushroom and its involvement in all of this.

Most people have never heard anything like this. In fact their whole paradigm of thought might not even allow them to consider anything like this. Then there are

The bleeding heart of Jesus.

people who, although they have never heard anything like this, find it to be interesting, yet go about their way, likely to never have it enter their minds again. Some find it interesting, contemplate it once in a while, sometimes have events that remind them of the idea, like a mushroom on a postcard, but generally pass it off as not important (to them). Others find it somehow familiar, and do some research on their own. Sometimes I run into them down the road of life, and they say something like "Hey, remember when you told me about that mushroom? Well what about this, or that?" And other connections I have never run across can be made. Then there are people that have heard about this already. I like running into these kinds of people, because it is always intriguing for me to find out what they know. Most of those who have heard about it have never eaten, or even seen these mushrooms in person. (Lots of Mycologists have seen them, and others due to their interests in mushrooms, in general, have heard something about it). Then there are those who have heard about it, and have even studied it enough to have actually eaten it at some point. Most of them did not know about the levels of effects, by dosage, and have experienced only stage 1 effects. Many become perplexed that they did not receive the effects they had expected and so give up on it, thinking that the identification of the substance must have been flawed, and look for something else. I've talked to many people that felt that the ecstatic effects (described in the religious texts) must have just been a myth. Some have experienced stage 2, and still fewer have been to stage 3 (see recipe section).

This suggests a spiritual evolutionary process at work. It becomes more apparent when looking into the Hindu and Buddhist texts pertaining to spiritual evolution. Through the process of reincarnation, advancement is made according to knowledge one gains AND the discovery and application of key tools for enlightenment found on different levels of the path. One other comment I should make before proceeding is that many things have been written in the myths about the experience at death, when the spiritual journey takes one to the point of going onward to the next level or incarnation. This threshold (of potential achievement) is preceded by the eating of the tree of life, or the drinking of the living waters. Such as in this part of the Book of Revelation.

> After this I beheld, and, lo, a great multitude which no man could number, of all nations, and kindreds, and people, and tongues, stood before the throne, and before the lamb, clothed with white robes, and palms in their hands;
>
> Rev. 7-9
>
> For the lamb which is in the midst of the throne shall feed them, and shall lead them unto living fountains of waters: And God shall wipe away all tears from their eyes.
>
> Rev. 2-17

It is interesting that even though these people have died (physically), and are before the throne of God, there is still this mention of the fountains of living waters, which the lamb will lead them to. This is done for the multitudes of all the earth. Who can know the real reason that even spiritually there is a need for this substance? At any level of understanding, it is apparent that the Lamb knows, and so guides the multitudes to the fountain which contains their reward.

Jesus in a "Tub" of Transfiguration

This 15th Century fresco shows Jesus with cross in a TUB that looks remarkably similar to the TUB in the central chamber in the Great Pyramid at Gizeh (This will be explored later). This shows both baptisms. 1) The baptism by water (tub) and 2) The second by fire (cross). The cross being a symbol for the mushroom. There are, after all, TWO baptisms. The First is baptism by water. The second is baptism by FIRE. This is the transformational baptism. The death (journey to the heavens) and the rebirth experience of the God. The mushroom has a long association (largely due to its color) with fire. High on the mountain-top, where the mushrooms grow, Moses conversed with the God who appeared as the "Burning Bush."

Christianity was the first religion that I studied in-depth after finding out about the mushroom. This was due to my heritage and upbringing. After four years (of knowing) I finally had my first experience. As you can see, from what I understood, I fully expected to see the throne of God and Jesus, the hierarchy of angels, and the whole works. But when I opened the door, ate the flesh/bread, and drank of the waters of life, I found much, much more. There was no Jesus (so to speak) there to greet me. People have the supposition that "as they believe, so shall it be." The more proper way (to me) to look at it is this: "So as you believe, you can count on being wrong." Because not only is life NOT as easy as believing in ANY God, or anything, it is a continual learning process that seems to have no end, and therefore, becoming stagnant, as pertaining to spiritual learning, is a dangerous trap for those who think they have found the one true thing they need to know in life. The world is consumed by the huge beast/spirit of deception (remember that one? The one that everyone inside their minds believes could not possibly have gotten them.) Simply believing anything is not the key to salvation. At best it would surely be thought of as "The easy way out." Neither is finding the mushroom and going in through the door, and being taught, one, two, or a hundred times, going to ever end your quest for knowledge and understanding. Think about it this way, even a God must be able to evolve or life would become boring. The first thing you learn is that there is no easy way out, that is, if you are interested in anything beyond simply being saved (not dying the spiritual death). There are many levels of evolution, spiritual as well as physical. When you open the door and look inside, you can see these evolutionary levels and that they are accessible, but they require certain understandings. You see them, and visit them, and know that they are there, but due to the conditioning that has been done to you in life, you realize that you must dump a lot of baggage to evolve into those levels. It is a very humbling experience indeed. Much of that baggage that must be left behind originates in the belief systems that are taught to us lowly humans by the religions on this planet. The political/religious organizations that alter the truth to fit their societal models, have polluted it, and thereby destroyed it. This goes beyond these systems of belief simply being a hindrance to spiritual evolution. These have become the great beasts that drag souls to destruction, by replacing truth with false morals and dogma. The Beast is camouflaged as the truth, in an a extremely diabolical and complex web. A trap, of which ESCAPE may be that very thing which human existence is really all about. Finding the way out. Each new truth dashing a dogma to the rocks. Each new revelation opening up (making accessible) another sphere/level of spiritual evolution.

There may be a reason that this mushroom has remained hidden for these many thousands of years. What has become clear is that, cosmologically, every religion on our planet looks forward to a time in the future where man will have direct contact with what can be defined as God. The thousand year reign of the messiah, the new golden age, the return of Jesus, Buddha, Krishna, Mithra, King Arthur, etc., is a commonality that is the hoped-for relief to the people that wish to live in peace and understanding. A time when all lies will be exposed. A time when oppression of the righteous will cease. A time that hinges completely on truth and reality, not societal restrictions of those who wish to control humanity according to their dogmatic and sadistic beliefs. This mushroom plays a huge role in the coming dispensation of this "Golden Age."

Sumeria: The Cradle of Civilization?

Now that I have written a bit about Christianity, I thought a good place to continue would be to jump back in history about 6000 years to Mesopotamia. The reason I am going to discuss this is that many of the religions which came into existence after this time period are based on adaptations of the mythologies/stories which are found there.

The stories and myths retain their basic structure, but the names of the key players have been changed, as they were incorporated into new religious systems. This is why most religions contain stories of the flood, the creation epic, the attributes of deities, and similar laws of government. There are many modern authors, including Sitchin, Gardner, Bramley, Freer, and Horn, who have written about the extraterrestrial connections in the complex study of mankind, and their so-called gods. Here is my take on the subject after studying this.

The clay tablets tell us of the Elohim/Anunnaki who were extraterrestrial beings that came to Earth from a planet called Nibiru. They genetically manipulated indigenous beings (which they called beasts), creating the human race. In the tales were the father-god, An/Anu, his two sons Enki/Ea and Enlil/Ilu-kur-gal, the primary male beings featured in the story of the creation of the Adama/Adam and Eve. Enki was very impressed with, and felt compassion towards, the products of this genetic work, namely "us," whereas Enlil was of the mind that the beings were only worthy of servitude. The ancient Sumerian gods, and their feuding ways have been found in later religious myths with the same basic stories, however, the names Ea, Enki, Enlil, Anu, etc., were changed to Ahura Mazda, Jehovah, Lord, Ahriman, Baal, Adon, etc. Biblical myths of Jacob and Esau, feuding over birthright, are similar to accounts in the Sumerian tales of Enki and Enlil. The Anunnaki, as a whole, were compelled to allot for themselves the status of gods over the lowly humans. The archetypal feuding brothers can be stereotyped and categorized by their respective attributes, Enki is also called Adonai (the "Lord"), and his (divine) attributes are compassion, wisdom, and fertility (sexuality); Enlil is called El Shaddai, The Lofty Mountain (YHWH), and "Jehovah." He was a storm-god who brought vengeance and wrath; he was jealous and controlling. Therefore "The Lord" (Enki) and "Jehovah" (Enlil) are not one and the same, but two different beings.

It was Enki and his sister Ninhursag who performed the genetic manipulation which resulted in the Adama (the ancient name for the first human, Adam and/or Eve). Humanity was conditioned to be in the service of the gods, but Enki had another plan which set off a continual series of events, which most adversarial myths, concerning the war over the humans between Enki and Enlil, were fashioned. Enki desired to feed the humans the fruit of the Tree of Knowledge. He knew this was the thing which would open the eyes of man, and multi-dimensionalize his consciousness. This did not go over well with the Anunnaki, and Enki was commanded not to allow us this fruit. It was Enlil who attempted to scare the humans into not eating the fruit by telling them that, if they ate it, they would die. Enki went against the wishes of the high council and was able to convince them to eat the fruit anyway. When the gods saw what he had done, they condemned the act and insisted that the corrupted humans be exiled from the land of paradise. Enki was man's preserver and compatriot, Enlil was the bringer of woes and doom.

It was also Enki that saved humanity from the flood, which was brought on by Enlil. Enlil also destroyed Sodom and Gomorrah, which, contrary to current precepts, were great cities of freedom and learning, not deserving of the jealous and controlling Enlil's destructive rage. Enlil is also purported to have destroyed Babylon, confounded the languages (after the tower of Babel incident), and wreaked havoc upon the city of Ur. It is extremely important to understand these earlier stories, as they were written on the Sumerian tablets, and compare them to the 4000 year later adaptations in the Bible. Ea/Enki, was the good guy. It was him who fed man of the Tree of Knowledge. So why the need to flip this story completely upside down and condemn him as the evil one? In the Bible the word translated as "serpent" is "nahash" (NHSH), which literally means to decipher, or to find out. All throughout ancient times the serpent was known as the bringer of knowledge (hence the euphemism "be ye wise as serpents") and the precipitator of enlightenment. It is this precise thing that compels us to look further into the possibility that the good-guy is the one that is condemned throughout religious writings for teaching freedom and knowledge. This includes the freedoms of plant usage/taking for enlightenment, freedom of sexuality, and even the freedom to not be subservient to those oppressive gods who condemn these things as evil. In the cuneiform symbolism it is the caduceus (the snake coiled around the staff) which is the representation for Enki, in fact it is his personal emblem. After Enki fed the humans of the tree, and was then effectively exiled, those who remained under the control of Enlil and the Anunnaki were then clamped down upon, in a heavier way. It was Enlil who was worshipped through fear, and in later cultures named Jehovah. Enlil, that old extraterrestrial who adamantly opposed the education, freedom, and enlightenment of humanity in every ancient Sumerian myth. A full set of laws would be adopted, the other humans were instructed not to associate with Enki/Ea or the exiled. So humanity received the first commandments.

"You will have no other God but Me." Enki especially, and his radical viewpoints, were explicitly condemned as evil. Control of the populace was priority one, to the gods, and glimpses of intelligence, or too much free-thought were "THE CRIME," and not likely to have been politely viewed. But disloyalty to the jealous gods was absolutely forbidden.

"You will work for six days and then have a day of rest." This will be a holy day, set aside for worship of the gods. Ritual and ceremony were to be observed, and homage to be paid. Refusal was forbidden, under penalty of death. The technologically advanced Anunnaki had no problem convincing the primitive creatures of their superiority. In their role as the gods, their word was life or death. An occasional display of technological power or just plain fear inducing events, easily kept the followers in line.

"You will not have sex without the permission of the gods." In a genetic experiment, the production of offspring is controlled. Perhaps the gods had no idea what kind of psychological problems stem from the repression of human sexuality, after all, they are not actually human, but, it seems, they just didn't care anyway.

"You will not covet the things that you do not have." The "haves" must quench the desire of the "have-nots" by making desire a sin. Even the desire for freedom. Acceptance of your present conditions being part of your lot in life must be held up as a high principle virtue, quenching high-mindedness as sin.

The other laws are branches of these basic laws.

Please understand that I do not make the previous statements lightly. The implications of what I have just written are dire. The reality is, the conditioning of the masses, perpetuated by religious organizations, has created and fed that great beast that has been so warned about. To state that the laws given to humanity by nearly every religious system on our planet are not the all knowing God's UNIVERSAL LAWS is heresy at the least, though blasphemy is a more appropriate terminology. However, I think there is ample evidence to show that some of these laws are not universal truth, but are lies that are detrimental to the development of humanity. Good thoughts and ideals are often used in cults to lure in unsuspecting victims, then the rules of oppression are instilled, cleverly disguised as good, wholesome values to the unwary.

What kind of a God is it, who says, "You are free to choose, as long as you choose to do what I tell you to do, otherwise you will be punished, for all eternity, for your disobedience"? Going back to Christianity, let me point out that when Jesus was asked which of the laws was most important, his answer was enigmatically "To love God with all your heart, and to love thy neighbor as thyself." This certainly shows a completely different view of everything. The love of God surely did not mean those driving the slave ships. What he is saying describes a love for something that is far beyond any Being that can be seen. That ineffable, invisible, indescribable God, which is within you.

Mesopotamia is the home of the fabled city, Babylon. The laws of the Babylonian king Hammurabi contain an old version of the biblical Ten Commandments. Although they appear to be based upon the philosophy of "The Golden Rule," many of the laws are completely absurd. The biblical laws appear to be, at least partially, based upon the laws of a Babylonian king. These patriarchal laws could not have been invented by Hammurabi, they must have been adopted from an older source, the Anunnaki/Elohim, and expanded upon by this powerful king. Also, some of the Egyptian "Twelve Negative Acts" are cast from the same blueprint. Initially, human law was probably a necessity in order to teach the concept of the golden rule. Some laws appear to be a sincere effort to promote this concept. Others, such as banning free sexuality, restricting freedom to worship as you choose, and the condemnation of a desire to have a better life and possessions, are clearly not. These are geared more towards totalitarian control of an enslaved society. The idealism of a patriarchal society seems to be that same old enslavement idea, only under the guise of the good law, and the delusions of some sort of freedom. Whether the patriarchal laws appeared first in Egypt or in Sumeria does not matter. It is the understanding of what these laws are really all about that is ultimately the crucial factor.

Remember, these laws were likely to have been initially imposed upon mankind by the extraterrestrial gods from Nibiru, who warred among themselves, had fits of jealousy over control and possession, and most likely did not have humanity's best interests at heart. They are not laws that were created by the universal, all-encompassing GOD consciousness which humanity attributes them to. The phenomenon of how patriarchal caste systems adapted the oppressive laws will be dealt with later.

While many argue that society could not survive without some sort of governing laws, the "Golden Rule" answers this need more than adequately. Keep in mind also that it was the opening of the eyes and mind to the knowledge of good and evil that was forbidden to humanity by these same gods. It's not such a big stretch of the imagination that the questioning of these laws (discerning good from evil for ourselves) is important. It is a logical course to follow if one is to consider basing one's whole philosophical understanding of life itself upon them, and, in fact, a full and unbiased investigation of them is in order. If a human sees for himself the difference between good and evil, he can no longer be told something that conflicts with what he knows. Obviously if man is forbidden access to this knowledge for himself, somebody must have something to hide.

The name Enki means "Archetype," which is precisely what he was, an archetype for the post-Sumerian gods. Turning to our anthropomorphising of the mushroom theme, we find more interesting connections – even beyond the above discussed fruit of the tree story. Enki AND his sister Ninhursag were the creators of the Adama. The red of the mushroom cap, as well as the juice, are anthropomorphised as blood, and figuratively related to as fire. The cap is also considered the female genital organ, as was the cup (like the Holy Grail) from ancient times, while the mushroom stem is the phallus. Anthropomorphically the mushroom is androgynous, in one sense, being one entity, yet having both male and female sexual organs visible. In another sense it is two separate beings, joined together, in the act of creation, albeit only the sexual organs are visible. Enki is the stem, Ninhursag the cap, the two are joining in accord to produce the Adama, anthropomorphism of the mushroom into the two elementary archetypal creators.

Further evidence is the substance fed to the faithful of Enlil and Ninhursag known as "Star-Fire." This supplemental nourishment was produced from the lunar essence, or blood (from the womb), of the goddess Ninhursag. It is also called "the gold of the gods" and even "the red gold." The Anunnaki's abandonment of humanity was brought about by the fall of Babylon, when Enlil sabotaged the city, confounded the languages, and allowed the city to be laid to waste. Some myths tell us that when the Anunnaki withdrew, "like birds taking flight," they took with them the 'Star-fire', or at least the knowledge of what the "Star-Fire" was. The priestly caste which remained, now under siege, needed to take the knowledge underground. They kept the process a secret, much like the later alchemists. This "secret" was the knowledge of putting gold to-the-fire – to create the alchemical gold, the secret of enlightenment. Real gold, when put to the fire, melts. You do not have an end product which can then be ingested. As we have seen "gold" is a polymorphous representation of the mushroom, the color of the cap-skin is gold (when dried) and also reddish-gold, AND it must be put to the fire for the process of decarboxylation (literally an alchemical chemical-change) to occur before ingesting it properly. So the Anunnaki's "Fire-stone" is another one of those substances which has a multitude of descriptive features – fire, gold, red, female organ, blood, juice, and even "nourishment that bestows enlightenment" – all of which can be easily understood in terms of mushroom polymorphous and anthropomorphic imagery. It is also directly related to the pineal gland, the tree of life, the manna (or shem-an-na, which the Sumerians claimed was made from Highward-fire-stone), the Greek ambrosia, the Egyptian scheffa-food, and the Vedic soma. It was the most secret and powerful thing known to the Anunnaki, and was not meant for humans, at least in the eyes of the Enlilian regime. But for our archetypal provider and protector Enki, and his sister, our "mother-creator," Ninhursag, it was something that we evidently needed. By the way, Ninhursag, in Egypt, is known as Isis, the mother of all the living, and therefore is the archetype of Maya, Mary, Ishtar, Diana, etc. In the *Egyptian Book of the Dead*, the pharaoh, who is searching for the ultimate food of the gods, continuously repeats the statement "what is it?" at every step of his journey. This question is the very definition given for the enigmatic "manna" in the Jewish records. What is this "Star-fire"? That which humanity has been forbidden by the Anunnaki, at least those Anunnaki which do not wish humanity to succeed, and in the case of Enlil, were willing to wreak all manner of deception and destruction to keep it a secret.

The Sumerian Anunnaki

The region of Mesopotamia (Sumeria), which seems to have suddenly appeared as an advanced culture out of nowhere (according to academia), had a high knowledge of astronomy, architecture, a pantheon of gods, agriculture, gourmet foods, and courts. It is considered to be the cradle of civilization. Mesopotamia, in the north, encompassed the rivers Tigris and Euphrates, which flowed from the Garden of Eden in the Genesis stories. The places known as Atlantis, Dilmun, and Lemuria are mentioned in the records of Sumeria. This is an obvious indication that these societies or cities pre-dated the Sumerian era. Therefore, the Mesopotamian civilization did not suddenly appear out of nowhere. It was more likely a relocated ancient "lost civilization," which, as we will explore, encompassed KMT/Khemit (Egypt), which is considered by many to be the true "cradle of civilization." But this would dash the academic world to the ground, even leaving entirely alone, for the time being, the possibilities that Atlantis and Lemuria may have actually been real civilizations themselves. Mesopotamia does not have the advanced technological relics that are found in Egypt, and therefore must have been a later civilization, or one which was not allowed this knowledge any more, as those technologies still have not been

The Sumerian Anunnaki.

reproduced anywhere on earth. Khemit will be dealt with at length later, but for now we look at Sumer for more similarities. A dominant patriarchal system of rulership had engulfed the society and its government by the time the Mesopotamian civilization was established. This patriarchy was later passed on and adopted to become Christianity, Rome, and Islam, as well as other European and western cultural civilizations. More than 4,000 years before the Bible, the stories of The Garden of Eden, The Flood, and The Creation (of the Earth, plants, beasts, and Man) were preserved, in cuneiform, on tablets of clay which were unearthed in the late 19th century. After years of research and translating of the tablets, those later Biblical versions of the same stories have taken on a whole new meaning.

One of the things that we, as humans, need to understand is that we must look at both sides of any idea before we make a decision. Otherwise we are truly the definition of the word gullible. This is especially important in dealing with the matter of giving away your soul to a supposed deity that asks you to surrender it without question and completely. And of course when that same supposed deity wants your service in bringing other souls to its fold, there is danger afoot. Be careful about that.

Religion preys on those who are full of guilt and fearful of death. The importance of finding one's path has led many into the dens of deception. So many people have turned their souls over to a God in the hope that they will not disappear when they die. The tactic of the dark lord of evil, whether manifested in Babylon or America, is to instill guilt and fear into the hearts and minds of the human prey, then offer a route of escape which promises your only possible forgiveness, or hope, is what they are telling you. So people surrender their souls to belief systems that put them into the position of going to work recruiting other souls for the same master. The surrender of one's soul to any deity is something not to be taken lightly. In other words, before you do something like that, it is admirable and prudent to fully research, from both viewpoints, the validity of the system and the documents that you are putting your faith in. This is the way to look at anything – to look at it completely from both sides. And even then, you may believe that you have found the correct way, the proper path, the ultimate reality, but surrendering your soul and recruiting souls just seems to be a strange requirement from any almighty deity.

It is simple to see that if you can control a persons sexuality you can get them to believe anything. Government enforces the religion of the dark lords. The concept of guilt, associated with sex, is an ancient tool for control. The oppressor says, "Sex is bad, unless I say it's okay." As in, "you must have a license to engage in licentious behavior." There are far too many forms of totalitarian dictatorship, with government-enforced religious law.

"Follow Your Bliss" remains one of the truest thoughts on religious freedom. Even with all of the negative connotations heaped upon it by religious systems (who want control), that are contorting it to be a statement of evil, with such pedantic reasoning as "So if I want to kill, it's okay?," they are ignoring the golden rule as the first law of following one's bliss.

Secret societies have a great motto – "Ordo Ab Chao," meaning "Order Out of Chaos." Agendas are formulated designed to give the powerful more power. Chaos is created, and media blitzed. Then cries go out for a solution. Laws are passed which could never have been passed without the chaos. The order has reigned, through deception of the masses, and the agenda is accomplished.

The fascist state that is being created by these secret societies fears the average person on the street. They fear detection and exposure – and being noticed by people everywhere that their religions, governments, and corporations behind this agenda are destroying humanity.

How can it be that a world so rich with resources can still be a world where poverty and hunger are still in such great abundance? Those who seek fortune from the exploitation of other human beings seem to be the pillars of the planetary hierarchy. The governments with their holy contractual ceremonies, the churches with their vast wealth, the bankers and money brokers who run the economy so the rich and powerful get more rich and powerful, while the poor are ground into destitution and the middle class collapses into obscurity. This very same governmental/religious/capitalistic hierarchy that is destroying the planetary environment, disguised as those very institutions that are supposed to be helping it, is grabbing up property ownership under the guise of turning public lands into preserves (this in America). This follows the very same patterns that have recurred throughout history – greed, corruption, and fascism waving the illusionary flag of freedom.

Freemasonry is the secret organization famous for its use of Christianity as a tool for control. The King James version of the Bible, edited by Sir Francis Bacon, a 33rd degree Freemason, is used to create order in society through the implementation of a belief system geared towards their fascist ideologies. The chaos is carefully orchestrated to insure the passing of more and more laws that will, eventually, completely destroy freedom. This is why there is more and more morality being preached by politicians.

Priests and politicians speaketh with forked tongues, out of one side comes the illusion of tolerance and understanding, while the other side says you had better believe what I believe or you are in trouble.

Just remember that freedom does not say you are only free to do what you are told to do. If there ever would be some kind of genocide where all of the non-believers would be put to death, this too would be nothing more than a recurrence of what has happened all along, on our planet. Fascism often rears its ugly head, and must take control of every aspect of the individual's life, thereby insuring that no one will challenge the authority of whatever religio/political image is portrayed to the populace. If, in fact, Sitchin is right, and the extraterrestrial gods did indeed plant the seeds of humanity, and these gods have been with us all along, then religion is right in claiming that "the Gods are ever present." Expected events will be more of the same old repression and oppression that has been going on ever since the beginning. Even in Mesopotamia, where Sitchin says humanity were slaves of the "Man Gods," who had power and authority, who kept the secrets of their realm to themselves, by saying, "Don't eat of the Tree of Knowledge," those who were given the gift of power seem doomed to prosper from the suffering of others. This does not need to be the case. This planet is filled with wealth, however, philanthropy and even kindness are always lacking. What else should be expected from those who find pleasure in the suffering of others? And this is the legacy of religion and government on our planet. If it's not one form of genocide, it's another.

Even if it means standing up to the ones that are in charge of this whole mess, somebody must awaken and do something drastic. If some expected messiah appears, but comes from the same school as any of the gods of the old world (especially those in Mesopotamia) then the world must prepare for another ride into hell, for as the world is becoming, so it shall become. The scholarship involved in the disproving of the world's religious systems is not an easy task, as everywhere you look they all say "I AM RIGHT." In my studies I have found that all of them are wrong. Especially those which are blatantly forceful in their attempt to control the human mind through false moral and dogmatic systems. The fruits of religion are frustration, depression, and despair, because they are bent on controlling the freedoms of thought, sexuality, and worship, including entheogenic plant use, and condemn real understanding. This is the current state of the systems imposed upon our planet. It wouldn't be so bad if we were just talking about rich people acquiring wealth and making something of themselves, but we are talking about a societal force deeply rooted in the banking, governments, and religions which is gearing up to instill a "New World Order" which will force dogma and beliefs on the entire world. Just as the people in Mesopotamia believed that they needed the gods, so do people today trudge along in their oblivious stupors, unaware of the mechanisms that are usurping all that stands for freedom. Active participation in society, ignoring the usurpation, is in my estimation exactly the apathy that allows it to continue full speed ahead. The destruction of mankind appears to be the nature, for some reason, of the patriarchal systems that took over somewhere around eight thousand years ago. Whether or not this is the inherent nature of the Patriarchy remains to be proven, yet by the looks of things, their nature seems to leave a lot to be desired.

Why is it that the idea is popularized (through media) that there are two things you should never talk about, religion and politics. This is because dialogue between people is the real enemy of the state, just as true freedom of thought has become "THE" crime. Discussions of religion and government eventually arrive at conclusions which are not in the interest of the authorities. Uncensored conversation allow people of different levels and fields of understanding to actually learn from one and other. No-one can expect everyone else to have the same viewpoint as they do, because everyone's paths in life are different. Some people know about this, and some people know about that. Its a big world out there and there is much to learn.

Anyone who tells you that the quest for immortality is as simple as one belief has not done his/her homework. People under this assumption might want to hold off on becoming the instrument of preaching that to your friends and family. It just might not be that simple.

Egyptology: Forerunner to Christianity and Source for Much of the World's Mythology

NOTE: Egyptology is really a dogma-entrenched and prejudiced study of the Egyptian theology. The true name of the study of the ancient land known as Egypt should be called Khemitology, as the true name of the land is KMT, or Khemit. This will be classified and discussed in a section of its own.

Egyptology and the Mushroom

Andrija Puharich, in his book *The Sacred Mushroom: Key to the Door Of Eternity*, describes hieroglyphic, and linguistic links to the *Amanita muscaria*. In his book, Puharich describes traditional Egyptian mythologies and how the typical (and obvious) mushroom pictogram and the ankh should be considered as symbols for the mushroom. Although much of this information was extracted while one of his psychic voyagers was in trance, this link has proved to be important to understanding Egyptian theology and, as we will see later, in understanding Khemitology. With the help of Egyptian associations to Mithra, the lion-headed god, the function of the granite tub (in the King's Chamber at Gizeh) is a key that will unveil the "Stargate." The Aten (winged Disc) symbolizes the mushroom cap with the mushroom gills being stylized as wings. The title of this book is profound, as the mushroom will be discovered as the literal "key to the door of eternity."

The Egyptian Scarab

This representation of the Egyptian scarab beetle contains symbolism for the mushroom. The wings (gills), sun-disc, and moon-disc. Look at this closely as you will see the same imagery used later. This is one of the views of the mushroom. Looking at the cap from the bottom,.the gills are prevalent. The scarab is considered hermaphroditic, or self-generating, much in the same way the mushroom regenerates. Male and female within the same organism, it is an appropriate symbol.

The central chamber is a place that opens the"Stargate." (Keep in mind that these rituals came later, historically, than Khemit.) This TUB is known to have played a part in a ceremony that was to prepare the initiate for entry into the heavens. The question is: How was this used in such a ceremony? A clue is found in the enigmatic salt deposits found all over the walls on the inside of the chamber. The ceremony induced an "out of body" experience, teleporting the initiate out of the body and into the stars. The Egyptians may have had a certain place in mind that this chamber was designed to help direct the spirit towards. Likely possibilities would be Sirius, or Orion. In our

The Egyptian scarab.

time, if one were attempting to recreate this journey, the likely desired direction would be toward the small portals leading out of the chamber. Astronomical alignment should be observed, as there is evidence that these portals aligned with certain regions of the sky at specific times, and that the initiate was thought to spiritually ascend through these portals. There have been theories suggesting that these portals were used to direct the spirit of the initiate to certain points in the stars. However, as it is thought that the spirit can penetrate solid objects, a guiding barrel seems an unlikely conclusion, yet all things considered, the jury is still out on that one. Buoyant salt water in this tub would provide a very nice sensory deprivation tank, for death and rebirth initiation. Much like the tank that was used for *Amanita* research in the movie "Altered States."

Initiation in the Great Pyramid

The Great Pyramid at Gizeh is the sacred place of initiation. This structure's relationship with sacred geometry, its effect upon, and possible manipulation of, multi-dimensionality, as well as strong theories dealing with energy production, make the enigmatic structure one of the most interesting phenomenon on our planet.

The Sacred Rite of the Initiation

The Egyptian mystery schools gave birth to other secret initiatory orders such as the Rosicrucians, Freemasons, Templars, and more. These modern societies elaborate upon, and use as a model, "the tiers of learning," which the Egyptian mystery schools incorporated. Mystic societies later perpetuated the systems, although in a degraded state, due to the actual pyramid not being used in the highest of the initiatory levels. They replaced the pyramid with a room and the sarcophagus was replaced by a simple coffin. Perhaps there are still those who recognize the value and importance of these artifacts and still do use them, but if this is so, it is not well known. The likely importance of this, were it to be known, to those who have devoted their lives to this pursuit, would almost assuredly cause them to abandon the symbolic replacements.

Those who aspire to take on the task of advancement, in the orders, are required to prove their worthiness through their proficiencies in the sciences as well as passing severe trials of various sorts. The ancient temple order initiations can be viewed as a gradual process of learning, accompanied by levels of accomplishment intertwined with secret oaths, which were rewarded through the revealing of hidden

The Pyramids of Egypt.

knowledge. The process of advancement was typically a lifetime endeavor, of which 22 years was the base period (according to Masonic tradition). This base period encapsulated the study of sciences such as mathematics, geometry, astronomy, and astrology (which can be more appropriately termed as astrotheology, as it was concerned, not only with the astronomical cycles and constellations, but the esoteric principles of man's evolution, and the mythology of the gods). Motivation for a person to swear oaths and submit oneself to such a long term commitment of study certainly has a lot do with an eventual hoped-for-culmination in the highest of secret initiations. Specifically, the initiation could take place only in the central chamber of the Great Pyramid at Gizeh. The imitations of this ceremony, in the later societal orders, are only a shadow of the real thing, completely void of the key mechanisms that make this rite what it really is.

This highest of initiatory rituals, in theory, is to be conferred upon those who dedicate their lives and swear their oaths to proceed along the prescribed path. However, in reality, the Egyptian mystery schools were supremely exclusionist in nature, as are the later societies. The true nature of this culmination ritual is obscured to the point of near complete extinction. Those who have dedicated their lives to this end have done so without the actual expected reward. Egyptian hierarchies seemed much more likely to confer this culmination ritual on those with the proper bloodline rather than those who rose through the ranks of the typical initiates. These initiate pools were more likely a sort of servile knowledge gatherers, and developers, rather than prospective initiates into the highest ceremony.

The Great Pyramid at Gizeh is thought to be the permanent record and physical representation of the esoteric knowledge of the highly advanced Egyptian (Khemitian) accomplishments in the sciences. There are mathematical, geometrical, astronomical, and astrological aspects which are all encoded into the structure itself. The anomalous energy fields associated with the pyramidal structure indicate the manifestation of multi-dimensional fallout, perhaps the tip of the iceberg in terms of the understanding incorporated into its creation. This utilization of the deeper forces in nature must be considered when contemplating the construction of the monument, and the enigma that the feat can not be duplicated even today. On the spiritual level, this multi-dimensionality has a far greater importance as it becomes one of the mechanical instruments utilized in the highest rite of initiation. It also demands consideration in many other areas, as the phenomenon of energy fields and multi-dimensionality open doorways of understanding and purpose that can hardly be theorized upon, let alone be explained in full. The surface of the enigma is barely being scratched upon – even after thousands of years of wonder.

The King's Chamber (Isolation Tank)

The ultimate sensory deprivation tank. The massive harmonic and energy-invoking central chamber in the Great Pyramid at Gizeh.

This highest rite of initiation, in order to be done in its proper method, is to be accomplished with the assistance of the multi-dimensional effects of the pyramid in conjunction with the multi-dimensional effects of the *Amanita muscaria*'s unique form of the death and rebirth experience. Another important ingredient in the rite is the sarcophagus within the central chamber. It is more than an interesting coincidence that the word sarcophagus literally translates as "flesh-eating." The mushroom is referred to as flesh, in most ancient traditions. The sarcophagus is where the initiate would lie down, during the rite, consume the sacred flesh, and drink of the waters of life.

The ritual itself, inside the Great Pyramid, was a three day long ordeal. It took place in the central chamber where the initiate was placed in a death-like trance. This death-like trance was induced by the *Amanita muscaria*, whose unique properties have been previously shown. Christianity, which owes most of its myths to Egyptology/Astrotheology, depicts this ritual as the mushroom-induced death of

The King's Chamber (isolation tank).

the Lord on the cross, burial in the tomb for three days (wherein there is a descent into, and a ministering to those in Hades), and then resurrection, after the stone is rolled away from the tomb. After the death-like state is induced, the initiate descends into Hades and does the work of lifting up lost souls through ministering in charity and good deeds. This death-like state is something administered by the priest in the ritual. The hieroglyphic symbol for "priest" is a horizontal line with a vertical line to the right, and a connecting 45 degree line at the radius. A pitcher balances atop the vertical line, pointing left, and a jagged line (like a river) pours out of the pitcher to the left of the bottom horizontal line. This symbol for the priest is similar to the astronomical sign for Aquarius. The priest is the water-bearer, or the one who knows fully and understands the true nature of the waters of life, which he pours out, or reveals to the world. The true nature of the priest is the one who can reveal the true waters of life (Soma) and can dispense this knowledge to those worthy of receiving it.

After three days of this death and resurrection ordeal the initiate is taken, at the close of the third night, to the entrance of a gallery where, at a certain time, presumably at sunrise, he is taken out of the pyramid, where the beams of the rising sun strike directly the face of the entranced initiate, giving him passage to the heavens. This was said to be initiated by the god Osiris (and Thoth, the god of wisdom) allowing the initiate to became as a god himself. Some theorists claim chambers that faced eastward in the Great Pyramid must still be hidden. Some theorize that the pyramid may be truncated, or the initiate may have been led to the northern opening at noon. Exactly how it was done remains a mystery. Hopefully, the theory presented here will spark further research and eventually this will be understood as it was meant to be.

According to Manley P. Hall, and also echoed by Peter Tompkins, "The candidate (the illumined of antiquity) passed through the mystic passageways and chambers of the Great Pyramid, entering its portals as men and coming forth as gods. The candidate was laid in the great stone coffin (sarcophagus) and for three days his spirit – freed from its mortal toil – wandered at the gateways of eternity. His "KA" (as a bird) flew through the spiritual spheres of space. He discovered that all the universe is life, all the universe is progress, all the universe is eternal growth. Realizing that his body was a house which he could slip out of and return to without death, he achieved actual immortality. At the end of three days he returned to himself again, and having thus personally and actually experienced the great mystery, he was indeed an initiate – one who beheld and one for whom religion had fulfilled her duty bringing him to the light of God."

Through personal experience I can see plainly the truth behind this initiatory rite. While experiencing the effects of the *Amanita muscaria,* one surely ascends towards the heavens and descends towards the abyss. It's interesting that the underworld in Egypt is called Amenta – which I see as accessible through the *Amanita.* The linguistic relation is astounding. The experience of the abyss is easily recognized as every atom of the self is dashed to pieces in the self-introspection and judgement that accompanies the plunge into that vortex, which spirals downward to the complete annihilation of the self. The flash of one's life before one's eyes leaves no stone unturned as each and every event of one's life surfaces into the consciousness. This is where one learns the humility of the adept, the infallibility of perfection, and the inevitability of error. "Judge not that ye be not judged" becomes ever so clear in retrospect, and the "heart that is light as a feather" suddenly becomes the most valuable element in the universe. The profound effect of direct sunlight, especially the sunrise, is something that can only be described as a "Born into the Light" experience. Each atom of the body can be felt to change somehow as the light, travelling through the body, can be distinctly sensed each micrometer of the way. Once it finishes its course, and the complete body is engulfed, there is an incredible "stepping through" experience, wherein the glorious beauty and ecstasy of the heavens unfold. This is an experience of the most profound and unique type. As far as I know, it is the only entheogen that produces this effect, and in fact this IS that proscribed experience that all the ecstatic religious writings refer to. This initiation ritual is certainly a prescribed methodology for the ultimate experience that a human can have. Knowing the up-and-down effect that the mushroom has, which is much like an elevator ride, reaching undefinable realms of the heavens, followed by a sudden plunge to the depths, then an up-sweeping again to the ascent, can seem random or at least unpredictable at best. This Egyptian guided experience, that holds one down in the depths for three days, then by design moves the initiate into the sunlight to begin the ascent, reminds me of a sling-shot. The further back (down) you pull the projectile (initiate), the further (higher) it (he) goes. This, combined with the multi-dimentionality associated with the enigmatic attributes and energy fields of the pyramid itself (the full understanding of which is NOT available to us – and in fact our understanding can only be termed as infantile at the present time) makes for an enigmatic voyage of the soul of man. The concepts and mechanics of these experiences have been locked away from our limited understanding for many thousands of years, beneath a myriad of symbols and relics. That it must have been known, due to the recurring cycles of the evolution of man, that at some point in time, the secrets of this mystery would be re-discovered, only adds to this enigma of the past. The prophecies and revelations of those mystics the world over, who tell of an ushering in of the new golden age, remain void of fulfillment. But perhaps not forever.

In the past, as today, the acceptance and challenges of these steps of initiation could have been the product of man's desire and search to understand the meaning of life, or the desire to help mankind progress, through diligent effort of individuals with compassion. These are admirable motivations. However, there is always the threat of a more sinister motive which is the desire for power. This dark desire seems to be the source of the obscuration of this entire concept. It is my opinion that those without pure intent (hearts as light as a feather) would be unable to withstand the powers invoked in the fullness of this true ritual. The results of which, for those dark souls, may be death or insanity. This failure rate may be the reason for the falling away from the use of this rite in its fullness. It can be demonstrated by the condition the world is in. After all, it IS those secret societies (which follow this Egyptian model) that control the finances, governments, and religious systems that currently plague the planet with perversions of truth and fascist agendas that are not becoming of the truly enlightened.

In looking at ancient Egyptian texts available to us today, we find many references to foods. These foods play an important part in the rituals of the ancient Egyptians. There are a number of hieroglyphic depictions of plants (many of which are psychedelic) on walls and within texts throughout Egypt. This is to be expected, yet this goes undetected or dismissed by most who are studying Egypt and its religious writings. This is very strange when one reads texts such as found in The *Egyptian Book of the Dead*. Here we see that this food is central to the ritual.

> He thirsts not, nor hungers, nor is sad; he eats the bread of Ra and drinks what he drinks daily, and his bread also is that which is the word of Keb, and that which comes forth from the mouths of the gods. He eats what the gods eat, he drinks what they drink, he lives as they live, and dwells where they dwell; all the gods give him their food that he may not die. Not only does he eat and drink of their food, but he wears the apparel which they wear, the white linen and sandals; he is clothed in white, and he goeth to the great lake in the midst of the Field of Offerings whereon the great gods sit; and these great and never failing gods give unto him [to eat] of the tree of life of which they themselves do eat.

> *The Papyrus of Ani* (The Doctrine of Eternal Life)

Now we can plainly see that this "Food of the Gods" has some major significance for the Egyptians. We can not overlook the "food" as also being referred to as bread (see Christian sacrament), and perhaps, most importantly, it is referred to as "The Tree of Life." Now it must become apparent that this tree was not new when it was adopted by Christianity, neither was it new when it was depicted by the Sumerians. Quite likely it was not new when it was written about by the Egyptians, either. What is apparent is that this relic was adapted throughout time by diverse cultures and religions from a common source. My speculation as to the specific origin is not important, what I am attempting to point out is the commonality of these specific titles given to this "Celestial Food," and the multitude of parallel references and titles of "it."

Let's examine some more things from the *Egyptian Book of the Dead*.

> Homage to thee, Osiris, Lord of eternity, King of the Gods, whose names are manifold, whose forms are holy, thou being of hidden form in the temples, whose Ka is holy. Thou art the governor of Tattu (Busiris), and also the mighty one in Sekhem (Letopolis). Thou art the Lord to whom praises are ascribed in the name of Ati, thou art the Prince of divine food in Anu.

It can be argued that this "divine food" is a mysterious thing that is inaccessible to humans, however, what good would all of these references to this substance be if it were not something to actually eat for the initiates? And furthermore, is there any actual reference to it being anything other than an actual food?

And again:

> May Ra give glory, and power, and truth-speaking, and the appearance as a living soul so that he may gaze upon Heru-khuti, to the KA of the Osiris the Scribe Ani, who speaketh truth before Osiris, and who saith: Hail, O all ye gods of the House of the Soul, who weigh heaven and earth in a balance, and who give celestial food.

Above, we see powerful praises given to the gods who give celestial food. Who is doing all of this praising? Certainly it is not the gods praising the gods, but the initiates who are the recipients of the food (from the gods) who would praise them for their gift.

Still again:

> May I look upon the Lords of the Tuat,[or, according to another reading, the Company of the Gods] may I smell the savor of the divine food of the Company of the Gods.
>
> Grant ye to me my mouth that I may speak therewith, and cause ye that sepulchral offerings shall be made unto me in your presence, for I know you, and I know your names, and I know also the name of the mighty god before whose face ye set your celestial food.
>
> Others, however, say that it is the way by which Father Tem travelleth when he goeth forth to Sekhet-Aaru, [the place] which produceth the food and sustenance of the gods who are [in] their shrines.
>
> Thy KA riseth up with the celestial food hu and tchefau.

Consider this explanation given in the translation notes:

> Tchefau, according to E.A. Wallace Budge, is the name of the food on which the gods lived, and may be compared to the Ambrosia and Nectar on which the gods lived on Olympus. Hu is called the god of taste, and in the papyrus of Ani it states that the gods Hu and Saa were created from the drops of blood that landed on the ground when Ra cut off his phallus. Budge states also that although it is known that Hu and Saa were nature gods, their exact role and part has not been satisfactorily made out.

We cannot dismiss the similarities within the above when we compare the phallus of Rhudra (Red Hindu god whose red phallus grows in the forest), nor the appearance of the mushrooms in the mythology of Odin, wherein his horse's spittle mingled with blood, as it hit the ground, and sprouted the *Amanita* mushrooms. Hu and Saa are again anthropomorphised mushroom gods (of nature). We also see another reference to the god being hidden:

> The God cometh forth from his hidden place, [and] tchefau food falleth from the eastern horizon of heaven at the word of Nut.

Coming forth "from his hidden place" is directly associated here with the tchefau food appearing from the heavens. Now there comes a very interesting passage which I will put to you (the reader) for dissection. See if you realize the parallel which I will draw forthwith.

> "Horus is both the divine food and the sacrifice"

As pointed out by John Allegro (*The Sacred Mushroom and the Cross*), Jesus has a duality. He is both the man (or god) and the mushroom (the food) and, of course, the sacrifice (the mushroom dying in order to be eaten). This is serious parallelism which must be considered when attempting to understand the passages wherein Jesus is explaining the "two mannas" in the book of John, and why his flesh must be eaten.

And more:

> Let the gods of the Tuat be afraid of me, and let them fight for me in their halls. Let them see that thou hast provided me with food for the festival. I am one of those spirit-souls who dwell in the light-god. I have made my form in his form, when he cometh to Tetu. I am a spirit-body among his spirit-bodies; he shall speak unto thee the things [which concern] me. Would that he would cause me to be held in fear! Would that he would create [in them] awe of me! Let the gods of the Tuat be afraid of me, and let them fight for me [in their halls]. I, even I, am a spirit-soul, a dweller in the light-god, whose form hath been created in divine flesh.

Perhaps the reader will not be so astonished now when I put forward the concept that the "Divine Flesh," which is being referred to, is the flesh of the divine mushroom, *Amanita muscaria*.

Now let us move forward to see what special abilities (or protection) is obtained for those who understand what all of this is talking about.

> [If] this Chapter [be known by the deceased], he shall come forth pure by day after his death, and he shall perform every transformation which his soul desireth to make. He shall be among the Followers of Un-Nefer, and he shall satisfy himself with the food of Osiris, and with sepulchral meals. He shall see the Disk [of the sun], he shall be in good case upon earth before Ra, and his word shall be truth in the sight of Osiris, and no evil thing whatsoever shall have dominion over him for ever and ever.

I have already pointed out that the *Egyptian Book of the Dead* is not exclusively for the deceased, but for those who die and are reborn (as in the death and rebirth experience) and is a type of map of the out-of-body world (spiritual dimension). The concept of coming forth pure by day (being reborn) has certain attributes. Coming forth pure could be the new understanding which is achieved through this experience, allowing the experiencer to shed the old guilt-ridden self and become new and pure. This is one of the things I stress over and over again, that true understanding allows one to shed guilt because it is realized that the guilt itself is caused by false dogma. The last sentence being "no evil thing shall have dominion over him for ever and ever" being the finality of true realization, wherein, no evil thing (false law or law-giver) will ever be able to drag him down into the pit of guilt and despair again.

Now we must approach a point which must be made, and understood, as to the secrecy of the mushroom and why it has been kept only for certain "chosen" individuals all throughout time. Many people have questioned "why is this a secret?" or "where do you get the idea that this is the secret?" Or even, "who are you referring to when you say THEY kept it a secret?" As I have said before, I feel this knowledge is now for everyone. All of mankind can now know and understand this, should their paths lead them in the right direction. "Seek and ye shall find" has more meaning when information is openly available. For many, this concept has gone unanswered throughout time, and these ancient secrecy-keeping ideas may have been the reason. It must be pointed out that this is the Egyptian version of the concept of keeping "the secret." With the celestial food playing a central role within the teachings of *The Egyptian Book of The Dead*, it can be argued that this is the reason for the secrecy (the knowledge of what exactly the celestial food is), because if one is to fully realize the meaning of the book, then the knowledge of what this food is would be a high priority. Therefore, fully revealing the secret of the book would be the revealing of the true identity of the substance (the celestial food).

Again from the Egyptian Book of the Dead:

> Let not the multitude [know of it] except thyself and the beloved friend of thy heart. Thou shalt do this book in the seh chamber on a cloth painted with the stars in colour all over it. It is indeed a mystery. The dwellers in the swamps of the Delta and everywhere there shall not know it. It shall provide the Khu with celestial food upon in Khert-Neter. It shall supply his Heart-soul with food upon earth. It shall make him to live for ever. No [evil] thing shall have the master over him.

And:

> Thou shalt not perform this ceremony before any human being except thine own self, or thy father, or thy son, because it is an exceedingly great mystery of the Amentet, and it is a type of the hidden things of

the Tuat. When this ceremony hath been performed for the deceased, the gods, and the Spirit-souls, and the dead shall see him in the form of Khenti-Amenti, and he shall have power and dominion like this god.

Much in the same vein as the "pearls before swine" parable, here we see specific exclusionary concepts pertaining to the book, the food, and the ritual itself. Herein we have overtones of the very essence of the Egyptian Mystery Schools. The secret oaths and combinations which have kept this mystery under lock and key for far too long may have had their time, but no longer. It is of course my understanding that this food is the central element to the Egyptian religion (as it is in many others), and the central and deepest kept secret of the many exclusive secret societies that were to follow in its footsteps. As in Egypt, so in the rest of the world, the mushroom (celestial Tree-of-Knowledge/Life) is the central (hidden) and most important element within religion itself.

And finally:

May the goddess Sekhmet raise me, and lift me up. Let me ascend into heaven, let that which I command be performed in Het-ka-Ptah. I know how to use my heart. I am master of my heart-case. I am master of my hands and arms. I am master of my legs. I have the power to do that which my KA desireth to do. My Heart-soul shall not be kept a prisoner in my body at the gates of Amentet when I would go in peace and come forth in peace.

He shall be in high favour with the king, and with the shenit nobles of his court, and there shall be given unto him cakes and cups of drink, and portions of flesh, upon the altar-table of the Great God.

Al Khemit: (Ancient Egypt) The Heart of the Lost Civilization

KMT or Khemit (Al Khemit) is the ancient and more correct name for Egypt. Much has been said about the Great Pyramid at Gizeh, and the ancient temples of the region along the Nile, yet even after thousands of years of wonder, there still remains a hidden and vast amount of information that research and study can not explain. One of the biggest problems in putting the pieces of the puzzle together is there is so much erroneous and false information about it, which is accepted as fact. The dates of 2,500 to 3,500 BCE given for the construction of the pyramids at Gizeh, and other structures in the region, should be taken with a grain of salt. Taking into consideration the proliferance of obvious dogma associated with nearly everything concerning Egypt, including the very name of the place, which is actually Al Khemit or KMT (Egypt being the Greek name given after their occupation of the area), it should be no surprise that much information is hidden about the true religious history of those North African peoples. It is a land that has been stripped of its history, religion, and even its very name by those who conquered and re-conquered the area. A perfect example of the prevalent dogma is the accepted Egyptologist's explanation of the construction of the pyramids. Two technologies/methods were needed and are described, in the ancient texts, for construction. One is that the blocks had to be quarried, cut out of solid granite.

The tools in the Egyptian museum in Cairo, supposedly used for this, are copper chisels and round rocks. Anyone who has ever tried to dent a granite rock with a chisel (let alone a copper one) and has seen the precision of the cuts in the granite artifacts, knows this is impossible. A round rock beating another rock (granite) is even more unlikely. It is known that some of the artifacts were produced by this method, but those items are obviously produced in this way, and do not show anything like the precision craftsmanship found on the sarcophagus in the pyramid of Khefren. In fact, the difference is obvious and astounding. Then there is the problem of moving the granite stones into place. The standard explanation of floating granite blocks on boats and rolling them up ramps to the top of the pyramids is dumbfounding. Some of the granite blocks, statues, and obelisks weigh in excess of 1,200 tons! That is about 2.5 million pounds. You can not roll a 2.5 million pound chunk of Granite across sand (or even a hard pan) with logs or anything else, period. In fact, the largest cranes on the planet can not even lift anything that heavy. These two feats of wonder, cutting the granite and moving it (lifting it into place), which cannot be done today, even with our highest technology, point to ancient abilities beyond our understanding. There is much speculation about E.T.'s building the pyramids, and speculation about cutting the granite with laser beams. This is another explanation that does not hold water. An engineer friend of mine, Christopher Dunn (author of *The Giza Power Plant*), has witnessed what a 2,500 watt laser beam does when it hits solid granite, and it does practically nothing! Anyone familiar with lasers knows that a 2,500 watt laser is

The winged Isis.

extremely powerful. It can cut through solid steel like butter, but granite is another story altogether. Those humans indigenous to the land of ancient Khemit who have passed down an oral tradition of who built the Pyramids, and how, may hold the key to unraveling the truth behind this mystery.

The Winged Isis

The winged goddess Isis, was the mother of Horus and consort of Osiris. Compare this image to the images of the upturned mushroom cap, the thousand-armed Buddha tanghka, and the winged scarab. The wings again symbolize the gills of the mushroom, and this positioning depicts the upturned mushroom cap. Many of the Khemitian goddesses are interchangeable, as are the gods, and are more like mythological titles than actual names – much like the word god itself is more of a title than an actual name.

There is a body of ancient knowledge, passed down orally over thousands of years since the land of ancient Khemit was a flourishing civilization, that has been preserved behind the scenes of governmental and religious influence. The first point being that the ancient Khemitian society was matriarchal. Actually the term matriarchal is incorrect, but it serves the purpose of explanation in contrast to the systems of society and worship which are patriarchal. Matriarchal worship is simply the worship of the goddess as the primary deity, as creator of all things, rather than the male aspect being the central object of worship. The female deity does not actually dominate as in the male-dominated patriarchy. Rather, the goddess is raised up in the spirit of love by the males. The concept of the matriarchal system, as a female dominating societal model, has been adopted in recent feminist movements. But the entire concept has actually lost much of its true meaning, thanks to those who try to adapt the obvious dominant position of the male in the patriarchal systems to the female. In the ancient system the female was the primary object of worship and veneration, yet the concept of dominance is strictly a patriarchal concept and was not an issue in the ancient cosmology. The female, though the primary object of worship, did not have the need nor the desire for dominance.

The switch from a matriarchal society to a patriarchal society, on a global scale, accompanied the demise of the lost civilization. An incredible mythology exists in the ancient Khemitian tradition that sheds light on the entire cosmology of the matriarchal to patriarchal shift, the cycles of human evolution, and perhaps the very reason why the mushroom is hidden from mainstream view. The mythology is of

The Djed Pillar.

the goddess Nut and her male consort Geb. The goddess Nut (pronounced Noot) is depicted as a female with her feet on the ground, arching forward and curving her body to where her hands also touch the ground. Geb is reclined on the ground underneath her. Her body is filled with stars as she is the goddess of the sky (or firmament of the heavens). During the day the sun passes through her in 4 stages, mid-morning, noon, early afternoon, and late afternoon. The last stage is when the sun leaves her body and passes at sunset into the underworld (Amenta). This is called the Amun state. There are five states of the sun during a 24 hour period. This cycle is transformed into a longer period of time that encompasses a sixty-five thousand year cycle. This cycle is thought to recur again and again over the aeons of time, the position of the sun corresponding with the state of humanity as pertaining to the level of enlightenment, or the direct knowledge of the gods present on earth. The Amun state, or the period of darkness, is where we are now in the cosmology of this myth. This Amun state is known as "the hidden" (which is what Amun means), wherein the true nature and direct knowledge of the gods is hidden from humanity. This corresponds with the matriarchal to patriarchal shift which happened around eight thousand years ago. The sun (or light of the world) is not in the body of the goddess Nut, but has passed out of her, under the earth, into the hidden state or the place reclined upon by Geb. The Amun (hidden) state is portrayed as lasting eight thousand years, which puts us currently at the end of this "period of darkness".timeline. In other words, the sun (the light of the world, the symbol of enlightenment) is about to be born upon the horizon and enter into the firmament of Nut's body, allowing a new state of enlightenment to come upon the earth. This must be accompanied by a switch to the matriarchal system. However the matriarchal concept

Amon and Amaunet feeding Horus the ankh.

needs to be understood in its actuality rather that as a shifted and superimposed form of the system of patriarchy.

The Djed Pillar

The djed pillar is associated with the cedars of Lebanon. Does this image look like a cedar to you? There is certainly a reason why this is shaped this way. Of course it is not actually the cedar, but what grows underneath which the pillar symbolizes. Osiris, who happens to be the god of the underworld, the god of the moon, of plants, and vegetation is connected to this symbol. Some say it symbolizes the phallic of Osiris, which was never found after Set cut him into 13 pieces and hid them. This makes sense, but for deepening reasons. Isis found all of his parts and reassembled them, except she could not find the penis. Using magic, she fashioned a penis for him from a living tree (or part of a tree) and used it to impregnate herself on Dec 21st (winter solstice). Osiris lay dead for 3 days (as the sun stopped its north/south motion), and on Dec 25th Isis gave birth to Horus. Other stories say that Set put Osiris into a coffin and floated his body down the Nile, Isis then found him grown into a cedar tree (djed). The djed was used in fertility rites and rites of passage for young females as a practice phallus. This is remarkably similar to the Hindu myth of Rhudra, the red god, who was murdered in the forest, his penis severed. As his revenge, his severed red penis returns every year as the mushroom.

Amon and Amaunet Feeding Horus the Ankh

The Djed Pillar and ankh combination.

Amon (the one with the feathered crown seated to the left), in this relief, is holding the arm of the initiating Horus, while he pushes the ankh into his mouth. Viewing this relief head on, Horus has his mouth closed (pictured). If you step around the pillar, to the left, you see an incredible optical effect. Horus opens his mouth wide to accept this gift. Amon is accompanied by his consort Amaunet, and Horus (ready for his travel into Amenta) is accompanied by the lion-headed goddess Sekhmet.

The Djed Pillar and Ankh Combination

The ankh and the djed are both symbols for the same thing (or perhaps 2 types of mushrooms). This ankh, with the imbedded djed, is a clue that they may have the same meanings. The djed that grows under the cedar and the ankh which is symbolic for the mushroom and the cross, as well as meaning waters and life, or "the waters of life" (the juice extracted from the mushroom), are one and the same. The ankh is often displayed as being poured out of vessels, in streams of ankhs,

Mushrooms in temple hieroglyphs.

which are interpreted as water. However, it is not just any water. It is the water which has the magical properties of eternal life.

Mushrooms in Temple Hieroglyphs

It doesn't take linguistic translation or interpretation to read this hieroglyph, or at least this part of it. This temple wall was buried for thousands of years and still manages to have some paint remnants. If you visit the website you will see that one mushroom is red and one mushroom is blue.

Single Mushroom Hieroglyph

This hieroglyph is located outside the exit of an underground tunnel which was/is used in a death and rebirth rite of passage ritual. After passing through the tunnel (which symbolizes the womb), one has been through a profound initiation, especially if one is fortunate enough to do the ritual properly.

Single mushroom hieroglyph.

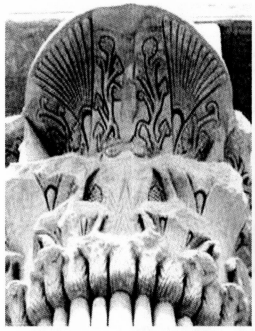

Mushrooms on temple pillar.   **Huge mushroom pillars.**

Huge Mushroom Shaped Pillars

The pillars which are at every temple in Egypt are shaped like giant mushrooms. These are shaped like the *Amanita*, some are shaped like Psilocybe. Others look like tree fungus and are decorated with pictures of an incredible variety of plants. As the ultimate alchemists, the Al Khemitians revered thousands of plants in their artwork.

Mushrooms on Temple Pillar

Here we have the top of one of the temple pillars which depict mushrooms. I cropped the rest of the pillar and zoomed in on the top so you can see the mushrooms clearly. Notice the similarity in this design with the 11th-century painting of Jesus, which I call "Jesus as lord of plants," with the four mushroom-type images across the bottom.

Ankh, Djed, Disc, Snakes, and Wings

In common practice, the symbol for the mushroom may appear several times in one artistic depiction. Note the disc (center) and compare it to the picture of the bottom of the mushroom cap, the way the top turns under all the way around the cap is shown by the outer ring of the disc.

Mithraism, a forerunner to Christianity, is the source for many of the borrowed myths.

Ankh, Djed, disc, snakes, and wings.

Mithras, as a lion-headed god

Mithras, as a Lion-Headed God

Many of the ancient gods transcend their respective periods of local worship. Observing their attributes, such as having a miraculous virgin birth, divine manifestation, purpose etc., it is possible to conclude that a certain deity in one culture is the same deity that is worshipped in another. The icon may have a different name, but was most certainly a new incarnation of a previous god. Cultural adaptation of myth is the norm, not the exception. This brings up connections that link gods from one period of time to another. Also, at any given time there could be several gods, all of whom had metamorphosed out of the same previous god. Such is the time of the inception of Christianity, when the new god Jesus had a rival in the personification of Mithra. A careful examination of these two gods clearly reveals so many similarities, that in descriptive terms alone they must have been different adaptations of a previous deity. Mithra is the same mythic being as Sol Invictus (Roman), Ra (Egyptian), and Surya (Indian), all of which are sun gods. The similarities between Horus (Egypt), Mithra (Persia), Chrishna (India) and Jesus are several dozen in number. It can be argued that if you trace all of the gods back through time, it may be possible to find their common origin. This original deity resides in the myths of the gods themselves, in relation to those aspects that remain the same. "Take and eat, this is my body" is THE central theme. All of the ancient god myths contain some sort of a sacramental food, and anthropomorphically this food becomes, at some point, a personification of the god itself.

Snakes and Stones

This picture demonstrates the button (first) state, as well as the intermediary stages, of the mushroom's growth .

Transforming out of the button/egg infantile state, the mushroom's appearance becomes more like that of a snake. Once the mushroom has fully grown, decayed, and dissolved it leaves behind a hole. This is due to it's pushing the pine needles or earth outward, as it expands. Around the hole is a white, powdery substance, actually the many spores it left behind. This hole resembles a snake's hole, or lair,

Snakes and stones.

Born from a stone.

which is another reasoning for the mushroom being symbolized as a snake. Most certainly, the depiction of the snake in the Garden of Eden, which revealed to humans secret knowledge that the fruit of the tree would make them as god, is a grand myth regarding this association.

Born from a Stone

The stone, small rock, and egg, are symbols for the mushroom in its button state. Snakes hatch from eggs, and as the mushroom pushes upward, out of the bulbous base, it is like a snake hatching, shedding its skin, and being born anew. In the figure we see that Mithra was born out of a stone, entwined with the serpent. This is purely symbolic, as no one would be literally born out of a stone. Instead, this reveals the god is the mushroom, which in turn is the god. This is the symbolic form representing the birth into the spiritual realm, through the sacred meal and prescribed ceremonies, again, a god-birthing scenario showing the god and the mushroom as one.

A Temple of Mithra.

The Temples of Mithra

Mithra initiates would partake of a Sacred Meal in their ceremonies, invoking the Out Of Body experience. An ritually designed sacramental, shamanic, and communal GNOSIS.

The Mithraic temples of worship, known as Mithraeum, are designed like few other temples on earth. Typically, inside the place of worship would be rows of bathtubs (TUBS) along the two side walls, or lined in two parallel rows from the rear wall to the front of the main room, providing places where many initiates could lie down during ceremonies. The TUBS were tools in the mechanics of producing a communal experience. The purpose being the joining together of the minds of the participants with the universal mind. The next phase being to exit the planet (physical realm) in a spiritual flight to the heavens (stars). This is a bold expectation to perceive, let alone one you can convince someone they have had, especially if after the ceremony they have not. Filled with salt water, these TUBS would become instant sensory deprivation tanks, much like those depicted in the movie "Altered States," that showed a group of scientist's *Amanita muscaria* experimentation tale. In this movie the experiencer digresses into a primordial state of existence. The plot is clear that this consciousness was exactly what the scientist was expecting to find. The quest is all important in this viewpoint, as the answers can only be given to the questions that are asked.

The ancients had a strangely discomforting experience when viewing a human body, at death, being consumed by worms (maggots). Their fascination with the process was symbolized within many religious pantheons. The worm is associated as the snake, as an easily recognizable serpent of some kind. The mushrooms go through the same disintegration process – as they expire they fill with worms and dissolve. Crocodiles were also mythologized as another recognizable cohort in their pantheon of animals. Dragons, too, are a product of this elaborated genera. This may very well be the reason for embalming bodies in Egypt, and elsewhere, this being an attempt to prevent the disintegration of the body and the resultant putrefaction by the worms. If there is something to mummification's preventing the body from being eaten by the worms, it might be, if you preserve the body, maybe you really preserve the soul. At least your DNA might withstand millennia of time, waiting for science to be able to reincarnate any person in the world that they had DNA samples from. But could they have been thinking about this back then? To preserve or putrefy, an option afforded to the wealthy, may be a choice reflecting a primitive knowledge of this possibility. Today there are companies that will freeze your brain, or even your whole body, with a similar purpose in mind. I actually like the idea of worms eating my flesh when I'm dead. I like thinking that the worms will then carry my DNA within them, as they metamorphose into flies or gnats and spread my genetic material across the planet, distributing it, eventually, back into the earth. Then again, if somehow, preservation is necessary for the science of the future to resurrect my long dead self, I wonder what all of this theology stuff is really all about. Just food for thought...

The Stargate

Here is an incredible artifact, one that is known as the

The Stargae of Mithra.

"Mithraic Stargate." If anyone happened to see the movie "Stargate," note how this looks remarkably like the stargate in the movie, right down to the symbols around the circular gate. In this case, the symbols are astrological signs. In the movie, they were replaced by anomalous, somewhat hieroglyphical symbols, location points in the stars. The religion of Mithra centered around the initiate's ability to communally astral-travel. Of course the out-of-body experience was facilitated through the eating of the sacred meal. After consumption, the initiates could traverse the galaxies, witnessing, as the ancient Egyptians did first hand, the reality that the spirit of the human being is not restricted to the physical universe, or the physical body, for that matter. This is the true revelation of the immortality of the soul, or at least the realization of such. This concept is so similar to the Egyptian initiatory rites, that it could be solid evidence that some of the hidden traditions of the ancients have migrated into later incarnations of various religious orders.

Eastern philosophy esoterica: The mysteries of SOMA and AMRITA, the efficacious properties of the magical/sacramental/transformational foods and drinks of Hinduism and Buddhism. The hidden keys to enlightenment. (The Enigma Continues.)

So many religions have used this mushroom in their sacraments, initiations, and rituals, that revealing this knowledge could perhaps achieve what many throughout the world have desired, a COMMON GROUND which all religions contain at their very roots. It is a basic common denominator which should theoretically bring them together. However, even though they did spring from the same source, there has been so much DOGMA added to the respective branches of the religious tree, which have focused upon derision and ridicule of the various others, that even though a commonality like this is found, there

James Arthur at Pema Osel Ling (The Lotus Land Of Clear Light), in the Santa Cruz mountains, California, 1995. Statue: Padma Sambhava.

may truly be no hope for this ever happening. First and foremost to this concept ever working would be the acceptance and revealing of IT in the first place. This would undermine the authority of religious figureheads, who rely on the beliefs (of their subjects), that they (or their religion) possess the only true authorized contact with God. By admitting non-exclusivity of this divine right to their supporters, they would be relinquishing authority, and therefore power. In my opinion, for this reason, it is not likely to ever happen.

The Flesh of Gold

The Mushroom itself has very interesting features that resemble, and have been related to gold, flesh, blood (and blood vessels), phallus, vulva, fire, saucer, cup, as well as a disc or orb. The mushroom has been, anthropomorphically, personified as a man, a god, something

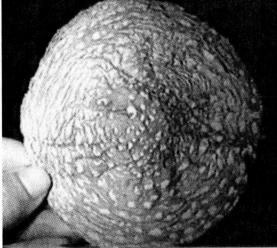

The flesh of gold.

of extraterrestrial origin, and a plant god, SOMA, who was mediator between man and the God/gods, in the ancient Hindu religious books known as *The Vedas.*

Hinduism: Soma the "Plant God" and other Symbolism

R. Gordon Wasson's insightful and inspired work, *Soma: Divine Mushroom of Immortality*, identifies the ancient Vedic and Hindu plant God, SOMA, as the *Amanita muscaria.* This was the pioneering work in a field that would be known as Ethnomycology. In about 1980, while discussing the inebriant topic with him as it is found in Christianity, Gordon told me that he felt I was probably the world's leading expert in this aspect of the field. This was a very proud moment for me and spurred me on to expand my research into even more ancient roots of similar myths. This is when things really got interesting. After discovering the roots and history of Christianity, then moving on to study other world religions, it was like graduating from college and then finding out that everything you had learned was wrong. Understanding the concepts of mythology and symbolism, realizing the political nature of established religion and society (with some help of the socio-psychology of Wilhelm Reich), were the next steps of understanding that transformed into leaps.

Churning the Milky Ocean

In Angkor, Cambodia, holy temples mix Hindu and Buddhist theology. Note the appearance of this beautiful structure, a megalithic pine forest, created in stone.

The pine (coniferous) tree is the host for the *Amanita muscaria* mycelium. As we have seen, this intricate relationship between the trees and the mushrooms was obviously understood and revered in ancient times all over the world. This symbiosis is a monument to the trees and the fruit that grows underneath them. The most sacred of all things is the elixir of immortality, which is Soma/Amrta, produced from the mushroom. Also sacred are the host trees themselves. This is why this incredible structure must have been created in the image of a great stone pine

Churning the milky ocean.

The great war between good and evil.

forest, fortified by walls covered with bas reliefs, depicting the stories of the sacred acts pertaining to enlightenment. The temple holds the history of great learning, the culmination of which is the knowledge of the elixir and its consumption. At the base of the pine tree "towers," inside the courtyard, is where the testing of the aspirants would occur, as in nature, where at the base of the pines the Soma can be found. Mix the discovery with the understanding, and the testing begins. The knowledge of astronomy/astrotheology was of great importance to many ancient cultures, and may remain so, especially if one is to travel out of body, or multidimensionally into the heavens. The fact that the alignments and positioning of the stars holds such deep importance, that it demands we search out all possible explanations.

The Great War Between Good and Evil

These demons are pulling the Naga serpent Vasouki across a bridge to one of the gates that leads to the Bayon temple (which represents the Holy Mountain), at Angkor Thom, Cambodia.

The gods and demons have always waged war in the attempt to control humanity. It is horrifying that one such war (between good and evil, as depicted in the myth) could have caused the complete destruction of this place. The Vietnam War decimated this part of the world, from which it has never recovered, and it's nothing less than miraculous that these sites are still standing. The acts of war and the governments (secret societies) that wage them have little interest in the understanding of the messages contained in these artifacts, other than the most likely supposition that they would want this type of structure destroyed, in the hopes of burying their knowledge under the rubble of eternity. The entire Vietnam controversy has been exposed as nothing more than greedy governments playing war games to instill a military presence that could take all control of the drug commodities in the region. The GREED and disgusting facts that this exposes is exactly what this type of story tries to convey. Good and evil are always at war, but the question is, who is good and who is evil? War is evil. The only good is that which opposes war. More importantly, who is pulling the strings of the puppets of destruction? Both sides are usually under the illusionary belief that they are acting in the name of good. This duality of purpose and belief could be easily exposed if thinking man would refuse to war, period. Do unto others as you would have them do unto you, and NEVER WAR.

The Gods and Demons

Hindu and Buddhist myths take on great form in bas reliefs, statues, and architecture. The Angkor Wat temple holds one of the most profound and important of Hindu mysteries – the manifestation of the "Elixir of Immortality." The churning of the milky ocean is a myth which allegorically depicts the spiraling (churning) of our milky way galaxy, and the precession of the equinoxes. The ocean is that on

The Demons pull the Naga serpent in one direction, turning the tide of humanity towards evil.

The gods pull the Naga serpent in one direction, balancing the tide of humanity toward the side of good.

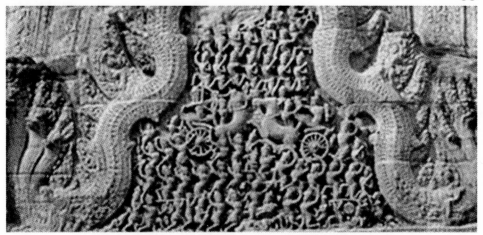

Those who war, caught between good and evil.

which the entire universe was thought to rest. This churning is the act which produces the Amrta (Elixir of Immortality). A high level of mathematics involved in the calculation of the precession of the equinoxes and the understanding of the spiraling of our galaxy, encoded within the structure of the temple, defies the idea that these were primitive peoples. The universe is called "the milky ocean." It is the churning of this ocean in an ageless battle between the forces of good and evil, which produces the Amrta (SOMA). Vasouki, a giant Naga serpent, is wrapped around the great holy mountain, Mandera, and is pulled back and forth to churn the ocean. As Vishnu attempts to steady the mountain by holding the serpent at the middle, gyrating with the tides of battle, the mountain is steadied to a slight wobble (which represents the earth's rotation through precession). The mountain rests upon a great tortoise, which is another incarnation of Vishnu. The serpent is stretched around the mountain in a great tug-of-war, in which two teams (fifty-four gods, and fifty-four demons) pull the serpent back and forth. This great pulling between the forces of good and evil turns the mountain like the rotor in a washing machine. This is the great battle in which good and evil actually work together to produce the elixir of immortality, Soma, or Amrta.

The Mushroom Disc

One of the many views of this mushroom, which is used symbolically in religious art of all types. Note that the center looks like the moon, surrounded by the sun, the representation of male and female.

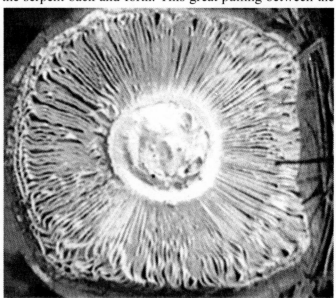

The mushroom disc.

Hari Hari holding the mushroom.

Hari Hari Holding the Mushroom

Hari Hari is a Hindu deity that is Shiva and Vishnu combined. Many times, Hari Hari is portrayed as androgynous (containing both male and female organs),

Bas relief in stone.

which is another symbolic reference to the mushroom. The mushroom stem and cap, anthropomorphically, are the organs of male and female joined together in the act of creation.

Bas Relief in Stone

A fine depiction of a mushroom disc separated from the stem, as the separation of the sexes. The phallic symbol is most obvious, while the disc-shaped cap of the mushroom is the female organ. The nymphs are worshiping the phallus by dancing in an enticing way to provoke the phallus to join them (the universal female disc) in the holy act of creation. This is incredible imagery – the phallus joining the cap to form the union, a sexual liaison, which is truly the universal process of creation.

Mushroom Discs in a Forest of Pines (Symbolism in a Hat)

A wonderful picture (bas relief in stone) of a pine forest headdress with specific mushroom imagery under the trees. This style is prominent in the Angkor monuments. It may also be, symbolically, a dosage requirement. Six mushroom caps of this approximate size would, in my opinion, be a proper dosage. There is a sort of fail-safe mechanism to this mushroom which has discouraged many a seeker. It is difficult to consume enough (and keep it down), of this mushroom, to get the desired effects. The amount you consume is all important. So many times I have talked with people who have experimented with this mushroom and claimed NO effects. Or at least not the drastic effects that were expected. I look at it as just another one of the ways this mushroom has remained relatively unknown, waiting for the time when it gets the attention and dedication it deserves.

Buddhism, Amrta, Reincarnation, and the "Wheel of Life" (Samsara)

Buddhism has been transformed

Mushroom discs in a forest of pines (symbolism in hat).

into several of the most mystical traditions that exist. There are primarily three forms of Buddhism; Hinayana, which is based upon some of the original precepts; Mahayana, which is thought of as the big-slow-boat to enlightenment; and Vajrayana, which is considered the lightning fast method (small boat) to enlightenment. The implement of choice for the Vajrayana meditation is the Vajra (Dorje) which is a metal object, round at both ends with a connecting piece in between, which is held and focused upon as a tool for quickly attaining nirvana. Vajra means "the lightning bolt which moves quickly," hence the speedy enlightenment. There is another element to this quick process which also relates to the Vajra. It regards higher levels in the secrets of esoteric Buddhism, attainable through the receiving of special knowledge reserved for those who are supposedly ready for it. Of course it is the lama, yogi, or particular teacher's prerogative to determine the readiness of each student. And it is also the supposed idea that the teacher is able to impart this knowledge to one who is ready.

Once again, we see that there is a hierarchical order involved in the dispersion of knowledge, and withholding of knowledge, which theoretically trickles down to even the lowly uninitiated if he is ready. The reality of this type of system is that it is flawed by its very concept of withholding anything from anybody. The hope of any student to find a teacher for whom their devotion is worthy must be determined by the amount of knowledge a particular teacher has. The limits of the knowledge of the teacher are the limits of the student. Teachers are never willing to admit they are not qualified to teach, so instead they claim to be all knowledgeable. Absolute and total devotion to the guru is an integral part of Buddhism, even refuge is taken in the dharma and the guru's interpretation of it. I point this out as a preface to say-

Buddhism and Amrita: Bodhisattva.

ing that the higher teachings of Buddhism involve the taking of the mushroom (the "death of the ego," yoga, or "death yoga"). A teacher who does not know about this is somewhere on the path to finding it out (as we all are). There is much to understand and study in esoteric Buddhism.

Of the several varieties of Buddhism, the lightning path method (Vajrayana) is the one that claims enlightenment to be possible in a single lifetime. The others, Hinayana and Mahayana (the big slow boat), speak in terms of it taking hundreds, thousands, and even hundreds of thousands of lifetimes to attain enlightenment (whatever you think that means). Now to me, the Vajrayana, lightning fast method seems like the most promising. It is this Vajra (lightning) that holds the key, and hence the very name Vajrayana. The mushroom's association with lightning has genuine mythological import. In ancient mythologies it was imagined that where lightning struck, there would grow the mushrooms (and some even still hold to this belief). Lightning, as mythologically used, is always a result of clouds, rain, and also that all important element for mushroom growth, water. As an example, Thor throws his hammer (mushroom) to earth and in a flash of lightning, accompanied by a thunderous crack, a mushroom appears on the ground. If it seems unlikely that the hammer represents a mushroom, a look at the hammer will back this up.

It can be thought of as the Buddhist Vajra, which also resembles a mushroom, and is associated with lightning. One needs to understand that this lightning-fast enlightenment is brought about by the death-like experience attained through the Vajra/mushroom initiation. Without it, the teaching and entire concept loses its very heart and soul. So, as I was saying, a teacher worth devotion will understand this, and those that don't? That's okay, because all are on the path.

Meditation and visualization techniques are commonly represented as a complete form of practice, and are certainly effective in themselves to a certain extent, yet I am sure that the different techniques were actually developed in order to expedite the processes one goes through while in the *Amanita* realms of consciousness. The centering, focusing, concentrating, and controlled visualization is very helpful when time dissolves, and the soul is put through the proverbial ringer. I have always heard stories of yogis or teachers of various practices claiming to attain the ultimate consciousness without any exogenous chemicals, yet it is extremely experiential, therefore, who can really say? It's like comparing apples with oranges, or better yet, listening to someone else compare apples with a fruit which they have never tasted. It also must be considered that all brain functions are the result of an electrical-chemical operation (not that all consciousness is only that), but dreams, near-death-experiences, psychic phenomenon, and visions have been linked to endogenously (naturally) produced chemicals within the brain itself. The two most common, Pinoline (an MAOI), and Dimethyltryptamine (DMT), are secreted by the pineal gland. This will be dealt with in greater depth in a later section.

The only experience one can really understand is that which they have experienced for themselves (especially in terms of enlightenment or portions thereof). Ancient Buddhist traditions that are still practiced today (at the higher initiatory levels) involve isolation in a cave in darkness. This level of initiation is known to produce quite the experience, but why? The reality is that when an aspirant goes into the cave (and is isolated from light) for an extended period of time, the pineal gland reactivates and produces the natural Ayahuasca (chemicals mentioned earlier), and higher brain functioning (mystical) results are achieved. This can be claimed to have been done without the aid of entheogenic chemicals, as none were taken physically into the body. But to claim that no chemicals were involved is highly in error. The same can be said for many other practices (including sexual ecstasy) which produce a plethora of various brain-chemical activities. So it is that each, and I would assume all, various practices associated with enlightenment within Buddhism (as well as other religious systems) have been developed to create certain brain-chemical functions, whether by endoge-

Tibetan Buddhist, Chakrasamvara, meditation mandala.

The wheel of life.

nous or exogenous means. This is the seed elemental concept by which all mystical experience can be measured. Chemicals are the multi-dimensional doorways by which humans achieve expanded states of consciousness, and even those states which are thought to be natural (and in fact are) must be considered electro-chemical in nature.

When I first started studying Buddhism I was extremely impressed with the iconography of the deities within the Bardo (Tibetan transition states between incarnations) because I had literally seen and become one with them. In fact, many times when I describe the various Bardo stages of the soul passing from one lifetime to another, people react similarly. They understand it, because they have seen it. I won't go into it too much here, but for those interested there is a video set out by the late Joseph Campbell called "Transformations of Myth Through Time," wherein he describes the visions within the Bardo quite exquisitely. It would also (on another note of expanded study) be very illuminating to read *The Psychedelic Experience*, by Timothy Leary, Ralph Metzner, and Richard Alpert (Ram Das) which is a manual based upon the *Tibetan book of the Dead*, wherein the authors explore the concept that the book is not only for the dead and dying, but that it is in fact a manual of the of-of-body realms experienced when taking LSD.

It is my opinion that the manual is exactly this – except that it was not LSD but *Amanita muscaria* which was the entheogen used. There are several others who have thrown some weight to this idea (and also, that it is the *Amanita* which is likely to be the entheogen used in the highest initiatory levels in Buddhism). These references include "Soma, Siddhas and Alchemical Enlightenment: Psychedelic Mushrooms in Buddhist Tradition;" *Journal of Ethnopharmacology Vol 48 (No. 2)*, 1995, 99-118, by S. Hajicek-Dobberstein, and *When Gods Drank Urine: A Tibetan Myth may Help Solve the Riddle of Soma, Sacred Drug of Ancient India*, by Mike Crowley. Both show extensive evidence that *Amanita muscaria* was known and used in ancient Buddhist practices (at the highest levels). *Amanita muscaria* is the Amrta and the wish-fulfilling-jewel, it is symbolized by the torma cakes and the stupa, it is literally the Vajra in Vajrayana, and it can now be understood quite clearly why this is considered the lighting-fast method to enlightenment.

Buddhism and Amrita: Bodhisattva

The Tibetan Bodhisattva Chinrezee, the thousand-armed manifestation. Remarkable in its beauty, this artistic depiction is not unique in its symbolic expression. Notice the similarity of the winged scarab and the upturned winged depiction of Isis (in the Egyptology section). The hidden symbolism is in the bottom view of a mushroom cap, the thousand arms representing the gills of the *Amanita muscaria*.

The Wheel of Life

The whole of physical samsara is depicted in this Tibetan tanghka. Samsara, represented as this disc, depicts the physical manifestations in the world and all of the potential states of reincarnation in which individuals are held captive by the lord Yama (the deity holding and biting the wheel). All physical incarnation, depicted within samsara, is considered a prison, of which ascension is the escape. This shows six states of incarnation, hell realm, animal realm, hungry ghosts (note that ghosts are depicted within a physical realm), humans, demi-gods, and even gods. Escape from the wheel of life is attained through understanding why one is held there. Through many lives and deaths (or death and rebirth experiences), one can escape by finding out how (through the acquisition of knowledge), one becomes the way one needs to be. This is good reasoning for the efficacy offered through death/rebirth experiences facilitated by the mushroom, and the process is quickened through personal revelation.

The Stupa, a Tibetan Ritual Meditation Object

The Stupa is a Tibetan ritual object of meditation. Notice the mushroom image with fire coming out of the top. This particular meditation implement is used in Vajrayana Buddhism, the lightning-fast method, which attempts a speedy process of enlightenment, as opposed to Mahayana Buddhism, (or the slow, or big, boat). This shows us, intuitively, that there are specific methods which quicken the process of enlightenment. Meditation, one of the methods used by both forms of the practice, involves a mental and physical process, during which one hopes to quiet the mind, awakening greater portions of the spiritual consciousness. Incorporating the mushroom into this process is one of the hidden secrets of Vajrayana (lightning-fast-method) practice. Meditation is taught at all levels of both practices, and is crucial to enduring the quickening effects on the consciousness that the mushroom offers. In my opinion, all forms of meditation (including Kundalini Yoga) were developed to help the mind withstand the consciousness-shattering effects of the mushroom and this is why this object is shaped this way.

Alchemy: The Prima-Materia (Prime Matter), and the Philosopher's Stone

Clark Heinrich's monumental discourse on the *Amanita muscaria,* titled *Strange*

The Stupa, a Tibetan ritual meditation object.

Fruit, delves deeply into the historical symbols of the hidden God, the god of a thousand names. Particularly interesting is the chapter on alchemy. The mystery of the Philosopher's Stone, the Prima-Materia, the decoding of the primordial mound and the Alchemical Hermaphrodite are revealed as the *Amanita muscaria* in this excellent (and entertaining) book, in convincing fashion. (NOTE: This book is out of print now.)

ETHNO-MYCOLOGY 4

This section will discuss elements in society that many would rather not think about or have to deal with. Inevitably, certain people seem to feel the need to oppress others in order to create more wealth and power for themselves. This is the dark side of human nature in its most destructive and despicable manifestation.

Secret Societies, Religion, and Government. (The Unfolding Enigma Continues)

The secret of the mushroom is not limited to religious beliefs. There have been secret initiatory schools on earth as far back in time as we can look. Secrets have always been synonymous with power. It is not hard to imagine, even in the times of the cave men, that whoever could make fire had an advantage over those who could not. Sometimes you might have a person who would share knowledge in an unselfish manner, but on the other side of the coin, there are many who use knowledge to control others through fear and the secrets they wield. Such is it today with those who keep knowledge to themselves for fear of losing their power. This is, in many respects, the same reason that a government would not hesitate to use a nuclear weapon on innocent people, to force their will upon those without the technology to defend themselves. There are those who know the secret of the mushroom, but, motivated by greed and harnessed by secret oaths and other combinations, they remain silent. Or worse yet, they actively work at the repression of the knowledge and persecution of those who know that which they claim for themselves.

Secret Societies, Government, and Religion

When I watch television, I see the propaganda that spews out of it like the script of a horror movie in the supposed NEWS. When I read the fascist propaganda that is in the newspapers, I know that this dribble is nothing but a smoke-screen to cover up what is really going on in the world of big business and government. It makes me sick when I find out that the executive orders that Bill Clinton and George Bush have written into LAW, are stealing the rights of every human being on earth (because the "New World Order" is already in that position) in a full-on acceleration towards a totalitarian dictatorship, flagrantly forcing the greatest free-world nation (and all its people) under the hammer of a hidden fascist regime. It seems there is no longer a world power dedicated to freedom and true human rights anywhere on earth able to stop the fully-implemented, corporate-run governments in power. When I hear that my friends and family's doors were kicked in, under the auspices of weeding out the evil people (drug users) of society, when I see or hear of someone knocked down, beaten up, and taken to the dungeons (jail) of the MAD Sorcerer's (police/judges) lair, then I smell the stench of FASCISM taking each city by storm, and it is not getting any better. Does anybody realize what type of world these fascist, prohibitionary governments are leading us down into? DANGER! DANGER! DANGER! The free world is being DESTROYED! Government must be STOPPED in their tracks and all laws regarding the freedom of human beings to put into and do with their bodies whatever they want must be abolished! The enforced societal model is flawed, sex and drugs are not evil, period. It is time for humanity to stand up, once again, and fight against the tenets of fascism.

The Fasces (Symbol for World Fascism)

The fasces is the symbol for world fascism. Fascism is wrongly categorized as only the tenets of Mussolini, or the dictates of Hitler, and in this way is restricted to these aspects alone. However, the fascist agenda, implementation, and execution is rearing its ugly head as the "New World Order." This is actually the same "Old World Order" as Wilhelm Reich adamantly described, thoroughly, in his life's work. The basic agenda of fascism is the control and domination of humanity, they

73

The fasces (symbol for world fascism).

aspire to these ends through the agenda tactics of oppressing sexuality, and consciousness/awareness repression. The implementation is through societal/religious models, and the execution is through governmental regulation, under the guise of allowing only proper (to the fascist view) actions, and enforcement of these repressive laws.

The Fasces, in the House Of Representatives, Washington, D.C. (District of Columbia)

FASCES: A bundle of sticks tied at intervals, with an axe handle affixed at the side towards the top. This is the symbol for world fascism. which is proudly displayed on both sides of the ROSTRUM in The House of Representatives, in Washington D.C. (District of Columbia) U.S.A.

If you happen to be a member of ANY fraternal/secret societal order, I have a few questions/comments that I would like you to think about. What is your fraternal order doing to stop the madness that is going on at the center of this governmental agenda? Do you even have any idea what is going on in the world? You're supposed to, aren't you? The base stones (of the political pyramid, which are you) have to get the hell out from under the other supporting stones of the governmental/societal pyramid, because it is each stone of support that keeps the stones at the top in power. A person who is a member of one of these societal orders is either oblivious to what is really happening to the world or is aware but not doing anything about it. Such a stone, by doing nothing, is supporting the rest of the stones further up. There is movement within the orders to stop the insidious tyrannical and FASCIST dictatorship which is emerging, or so I hear, but I see nothing happening that could actually stop it. I do not even see anyone in the forefront of any movement that is saying anything about what FASCISM actually is. The things I mentioned above are those things which you must expect to hear from anyone who actually understands what is going on. Even those who seem to be aware of what is happening here, and speak as if they oppose it, would only replace it with their own form of fascism, sugar-coated as a NEW morality, getting back to family and traditional values, which is that same old concept which feeds the fascist agenda again.

SHEEP: Are good for two things; being fleeced and led to slaughter.

FISH: Take it all in; hook, line, and sinker.

Both are easy prey for the guilt ridden, accusatory, finger-pointing, highest order of true EVIL: The Televangelist.

Do the secrets of Freemasonry really have anything to do with any philosophy or truth? Or is it just a social order to keep group ties stronger? The group ties only keep those who control the agenda stronger, the rest of the members only are allowed to believe they are stronger. The secrets may be there, but they are reserved for those who fit a certain profile, and the rest are only allowed to know those things which will keep them supporting the members who are ranked above them. These are the fascist agenda societal morals and dogma of the big lie.

The fasces, in the House Of Representatives, Washington, D.C. (District of Columbia)

Revealing the secrets of Entheogens, which is one of the most closely guarded secrets of Freemasonry (as well as many other secret societies), is something that can only be done by a layman (non-member). This is because if you have initiation at that level you could not discuss it any further. Secret societies are called "secret societies" because they keep certain secrets. I have spoken personally with High Priests and Bishops (secret society initiates), who told me that they simply could NOT discuss anything with me because of their oaths of secrecy. In fact they were so blown away that I knew the information, that it scared the hell out of them. Entheogens, and particularly the *Amanita muscaria*, are a HUGE secret. The initiatory rites, into this particular field, are so far up the totem pole of secret societies and religions that when you find those who know, they really freak out because someone else knows, and it cuts to the deepest recesses of their self perceived spirituality, and cuts to the center of their most secret God-given indoctrination experiences. They have this certain look in their eyes, and unless you somehow are perceived as a threat to them, they invariably have the need to tell you that they DO know what you are talking about (which is likely a violation of oath in itself), but they CAN NOT discuss it further. This has left me not only feeling disenfranchised, but sometimes pretty upset – which has led to some severe, yet moderated, chastisement from me. Actually, I have nothing against any of those initiates that I have spoken with, personally (including those that knew about it), but secrecy itself is a problem of high proportional magnitude, in regards to the reason this world is in the state which it is in.

In my opinion, the oaths and secret combinations are the basis for that which is fanatical, control-oriented and destructive. Secretive vows are one of the biggest

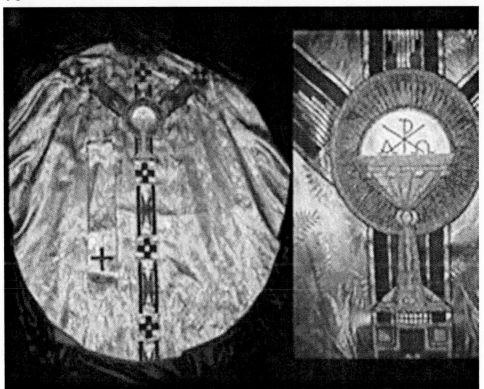

Clothing full of symbolism: A Catholic first communion robe.

reasons that society has degraded. Supposed truth should be revealed to all for open debate. It is in this way that evolution is enhanced, instead of inhibited. The secret societies strive to acquire information, technology, etc., and then hoard it for themselves. They then systematically destroy all public remnants of it, so they can keep it exclusive. This is a major problem for the world; it's like the Christians burning the libraries of the east (after pillaging what they wanted) in an attempt to erase the knowledge, and history, from the public domain forever. This secrecy is an abomination that makes the rest of the world desolate. Just as in the case of religion, where the revealing of the truth would relinquish the churches (and their authorities) of their power over people, so too would the governments and secret societies lose their power, were the truth to be revealed. And finally, those formerly oppressed humans would not take it lightly that their lives have been manipulated through the false morals and dogma of fascism.

Clothing Full of Symbolism, a Catholic First-Communion Robe

The symbolism of the cup, such as on this Catholic communion robe, is purported to be symbolic for the communion only in the sense that the priest has the authority to turn wine to blood, or bread to body. It is strange that the colors, shape, and imagery of the symbolism is so mushroom-like, or is it? This symbolism is actually not meant to be understood, at least beyond the dogmatic level, except by the very few elite. Which does not include the local pastor, bishop, or priest – this is secret knowledge of the highest order.

Alpha and Omega: The Beginning and the End

It is no coincidence that the gods said "I am Alpha and Omega, the beginning and the end," for it is in this image that all things may have been created, and in this image that all things may end.

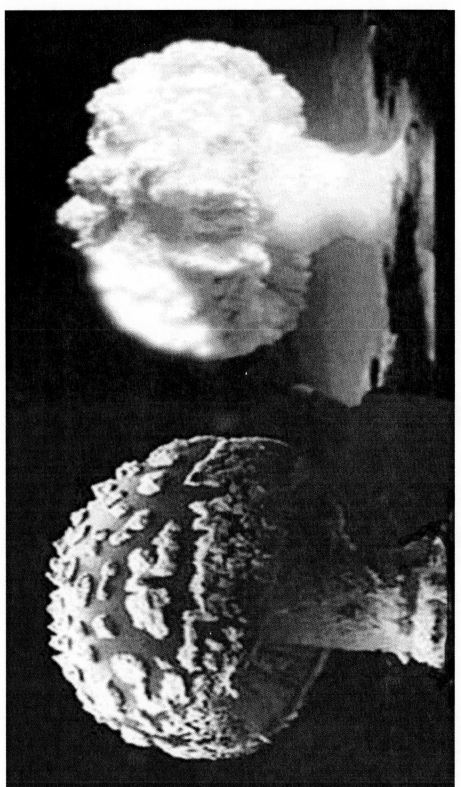

Alpha and omega: the beginning and the end.

Mithra, inside the "cosmic egg."

Mithra, Inside the "Cosmic Egg"

Mithra is said to have emerged from a "cosmic egg," depicted here in this stylized carving. In many cases the "cosmic egg" represents the original universe.

The Sacred Initiatory Sacrament

This one picture sums up many of the concepts that we have discussed so far. The angel is holding a mushroom, which is depicted going into the sacramental cup with fire coming out of it. There is another angel holding a fire container, which could be used as a cooking apparatus. This is similar to the Egyptian depictions of preparing the celestial food, and it is also very easy to see that alchemical representations have much in common with this early work. In a color representation of this image (found on my website), please note the five colors present in the angels: red, blue, green, yellow, and white. This is a common motif that will be seen in the next piece, as well, and explored more thoroughly.

The Sacred Gateway as it should be Depicted

Just as an entrance to the "Holy of Holies" should be represented, this arching doorway is incredible in its obvious symbolic allusion. After all, the REAL secret of the doorway, to the presence of the gods, is that which takes one literally into the other world, which is where they reside.

Jesus, Depicted as the Lord of Magickal Plants

Christianity claims to possess the express route to God, and exclusivity to the heavenly realms, yet this idea can be found imbedded and hidden inside most every religious system on our infantile planet. If (and I say this only to be objective) there is validity to any or all of these ancient, and not so ancient, traditions; it must be found in the real meat of the concept and actuality of the existence of an "other

The sacred initiatory sacrament.

world," and this meat must actually be able to produce access to that world. Regardless of what religion we may choose to study, the basic search is the same – a search for a spiritual existence which is best experienced, and understood, in the way it originally was meant to be understood – through direct experience of those higher states of consciousness, and communion with those entities, which are existing within the realm of that which many label as God.

First hand understanding is through the ingestion of the holy substance, of which there has been so much written that this brief *expose* merely scratches the surface. It IS this direct communal contact, which is truly the means whereby a human being can experience his true spiritual nature. One must take very seriously his or her own spirituality, for this is that which we truly are. As I stated in the opening sentence, "This experience is of extremely GREAT value." So much so, that I feel it necessary to the evolutionary process of each and every individual, and

The sacred gateway as it should be depicted.

inevitably to all of mankind. A careful look at this color picture (as can be seen on the book cover) with Jesus above the four plants underscored by the green vine, reveals much more than is on the surface. This may be an alchemical recipe for the ingredients of the true Soma (or whatever you want to call the elixir of the gods).

The red plant on the right is clearly the *Amanita muscaria* (which produces the quickening of the spirit). The next is clearly another mushroom, but it is blue. This would indicate a Psilocybe species (which opens the third eye). Next, we may have the depiction of the Syrian Rue plant, and pod, which happens to match this depiction in color as well as structure (Syrian Rue contains Telepathine, an MAO inhibitor, which increases the properties of the other compounds). Also note that Rue is likely to possess other qualities. The Syrian Rue (*Peganum harmala*) is an MAO Inhibitor which parallels the function of Pinoline (a natural MAO Inhibitor), naturally produced by the pineal gland. The combination of the pineal-secreted DMT (Dimethyltryptamine) and Pinoline (the MAO Inhibitor) may be responsible for naturally occurring psychic experiences as well as UFO contact visualizations. Fourth is a depiction of the opium poppy (the euphoria this plant induces enables one to relax enough to let go, which otherwise is a very difficult thing to do in order to fully experience the visionary state of this intensive plant combination). Fifth is the green vine which underscores the other four. I suggest that this may represent green plants, including Cannabis (which is used to prevent nausea and also enhances other things, as well as reactivating neuropathways opened by entheogens), as well as other green plants which have a history of indigenous usage the world over, including various grasses and plants which contain DMT (Dimethyltryptamine). It has already been shown through the research of Jace Callway, and others, that DMT-containing plants are mixed in brews with MAO Inhibitor-containing plants (Banasteriopsis Cappi, Syrian Rue etc.), to produce entheogenic brews such as Ayahuasca. These plants must be used in combination, as their psychoactivity, individually, is limited. This mixture mimics the DMT-Pinoline combination naturally produced by the pineal gland (in the brain).

So we have five plants (four specific plants and a fifth group of plants) depicted in one picture, but understanding why each plant could play an important part in inducing the ultimate brew may be the key to unlocking the mystery of Soma. The problem in concluding the discussion of what exactly Soma was, rests in the

Jesus, depicted as the Lord of magickal plants.

disappointment in the experience achieved by each of the candidates thus far proposed individually. This mystery may not be as unsolvable as it seems. The Soma brew was obviously a mixture of several plants. The case presented for the *Amanita muscaria*, by Wasson and others, is very convincing, yet it is certainly not the end of the story. As you can see by the research done in this work alone, there is ample evidence that the mushroom fits as an answer to the mystery in many ways. Recently, a book by Flattery and Schwartz makes a good case for Syrian Rue as their candidate of choice. Terence McKenna and others have exhaustively covered the ecstatic visionary states produced by the Psilocybin mushrooms, and their validity as a candidate can not be discounted, nor should it be. McKenna speaks on this with authority although he, like many others, considers the question unsolved at present (this current theory yet to be commented upon). The opiate-containing

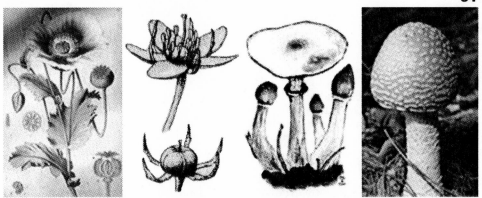

A mixture of these four plants may have been in ancient SOMA.

poppies, as far as I know, have not been singled out as a candidate,. I feel, primarily due to the overwhelming evidence for the other proposed plants. However, the name *Papaver somniferum* has a big connection, which the others (the Harmala/Haoma relation excepted) do not. Soma and somniferum have interesting linguistic links. Consider Somnambulism (sleep-disease), which, interestingly, is when the DMT and Pinoline (discussed above) are excreted by the pineal gland, during sleep. The answer could be that none of those proposed candidates for the ancient ecstasy-producing food/drink of the gods is wrong. After reading the descriptions in the various religious texts, each candidate individually falls short of the mark in producing the described state of consciousness expected. However, a mixture of these five plants, in this picture, may produce this long sought after and mysterious experience, which has remained an enigma for so many years.

Mike Crowley postulates in his work on *Amanitas* in Buddhism/Hinduism:

> "Many Vajrayana rituals call for the "five amritas." Could these have been five separate constituents of a psychoactive concoction? In passing it may be worth mentioning that the Tibetan word for Cannabis and its drug products is So.Ma.Ra.Dza. This appears to be a direct borrowing from the Sanskrit soma-raja (Eng.: "King soma," "Royal soma"). The term soma-raja is glossed as "king soma, the moon" in Monier-Williams' Sanskrit dictionary although the Rig Veda, in its hymns of praise to the drug, refers to it frequently as "King soma" (8.48.8, 8.79.8 etc.) (O'Flaherty, pp. 121, 135, et passim.). It would thus appear that either Cannabis was used as a soma-substitute or that the identification of soma with psychoactive plants in general was once recognized in India and that this tradition is preserved in Tibet."

After all; all roads DO NOT lead to Rome. Different "KEYS" open different doorways, and different combinations open different locks. Do not fall into the trap of thinking that any experience is the same as any other. This is NOT the reality of plant entheogens. A chemical is (after all) a chemical, but it is not just any chemical, it is designated a name to distinguish it from all others. Pictured above are four of the plant sources which I think to be the admixture called SOMA (the same as depicted in the 12th century art above). Excluded is Cannabis, and the other green plant candidates. Left to right: Opium, Syrian Rue, Psilocybe (wonderful painting, courtesy of "The Ones That Stain Blue"), and *Amanita muscaria*. four plants pictured, five colors,with green shown as if enclosing the others from below. This five color theme recurs in many mystical traditions.

Shamanistic Studies

A look into world mythologies reveals numerous claims of beings that have ascended beyond death into a spiritual dimension – a spiritual realm which is attainable through a quest, or search, for that illusive elixir of immortality. By virtue of this being so cosmopolitan throughout ancient documents, it appears to be of extreme importance to this life-quest. Also we must assume an historically common source, which appears to be the indigenous natural practice of shamanism. This dates from before man could even write, let alone establish any sort of organized religion. Those primitive humans fortunate enough to happen upon plants that expanded consciousness suddenly became aware of something beyond the normal physical reality. This realization must have developed a new contemplation of death and a desire for the individual to achieve immortality, and even to have a type of mythic hero's adventure along the way. This ascension-beyond-death-mythology is also frequently found in the same context as plant entheogens, which produce the "death experience" (the function of the elixir). This receiving of the death experience, to conquer death spiritually, is the core study and practically the definition of shamanism. This is especially true when compared to most spiritual traditions which downplay, repress, or otherwise completely obscure any and all references to the usage of entheogenic plants within the doctrinal belief system they profess to practice. This, in itself, is the core of the oppression of the natural indigenous spirituality, as it is, in its full fruition. The religious and societal oppression must be recognized as dogmatic and repressive in nature, exposing the suppression of diverse individual human drives and fulfillment. This suppression replaces our natural instincts to expand consciousness, enlighten awareness, experience plant substances, sexuality, rhythmic dance, and trance, with a societal model of moral judgements towards the freedom of these expressions, condemning them as a universal truth, and usurping authority to relinquish them to the nature of soul condemning sin.

The nature of the hero's journey towards immortality is also associated with the search for an ultimate truth, and finding it is a necessary step toward this goal of immortality. This also is a step taken in shamanism, which the plant entheogens are known to teach, if one is able to understand. It is this teaching which must strip away that which is in conflict with the natural indigenous makeup of the individual seeker's belief system. Tuning the mind towards the higher frequency vibrations must be accomplished in order to conquer death on a spiritual (which is also a physical) level. When the physical body dies, the spirit is thought to wake – but only if the hero is able to make this happen. This is the practice of shamanism, the journey into the death experience, the deep psychological introspection/judgement through plant induced states in preparation for the inevitability of the ultimate event, the crowning glory of life itself, death. This is at the forefront of the shamanic practice rather than a quest relegated to the deity one worships. It resides at the core of individual experience.

One experiences heaven and hell, and all points in-between. The hell being mostly experienced as one recognizes and then rejects (sometimes kicking and screaming) the deceptions accepted into one's cosmological belief system. This is especially true when these beliefs are deeply imbedded through years of societal conditioning, and are in direct contradiction with the indigenous spiritual nature of man. They become a second nature thought process, of which everything "one believes" is relied upon, as the self-manifested, yet culturally conditioned foundation of existence. Much of the conflict between culturally imbedded belief and the naturally experienced indigenous nature of humanity revolves around sexuality. Freud was adamant in his thesis, wherein society must suppress, repress, and fully denunciate the instinctual drives in order for cultural advancement (this is recognition of the motivation behind patriarchal systems). According to Wilhelm Reich:

> Freud's basic idea is that cultural achievements result from sublimated sexual energy, indicating that sexual suppression, or repression, is an indispensable factor in establishing any culture. Now there is already historical proof that this concept is erroneous, for there are highly cultured societies in which sexual suppression is non-existent

and whose members enjoy completely free sexual lives. Thus is the nature of indigenous societies. It was precisely my attempts at a sex-political criticism of culture that gave weight to our very first differences of opinion.

Wilhelm Reich was talking about the very oppression of humanity's indigenous and natural spirituality through an attack on individual freedom at its root source, sexuality. Freud's concept is a simple description of patriarchal, sex-negative, entheogen denying, religious systems. That philosophy is carried forward and enforced by governmental regulation. A clear separation of church and state certainly must excise any attempt toward governmental sexual regulation, outside the scope of rape. And the same must not regulate the ingestion of plant entheogens, which are spiritual in nature. It is the very nature of the established religious and political bond which perpetuates the sex-negative, consciousness-repressive society. This repression of mind and body, enforced by religious/governmental genocide against all who resist their attempts at conversion, is exactly that life-force in human beings which is crying out from the past for retribution and reestablishment as the true spiritual human nature is removed from exile. It is also always the quest of the hero to free friends, family, and the world from an oppressive, damaging tyrant or government. Of course one must first recognize that the tyranny exists, and why. This is the quest that must be carried on, and it should not be taken lightly. It is not an easy task, ever, yet it is the quest of every human incarnated. The degree to which one accepts the task is oftentimes determined by how much a person is aware of their surroundings, the repressive nature of their environment, and whether or not they possess, and are not afraid to express, a sincere desire to do something about it. It is the very deep conditioning and abstract, yet convincing supposed logic, that holds grip upon most of the culturally initiated in order to keep them in tow as faithful servants of that very nature which creates spiritual conflict, and forces beings into reincarnation. Spiritual death is that which consumes those who are not in contact with indigenous spirituality (which incorporates full individual freedom) but choose, consciously or unconsciously, to be the repressed and the repressors. Wilhelm Reich was imprisoned, died mysteriously thereafter, and his books confiscated and burned in the incinerators in New York by the FDA in an attempt to stamp out once again the uprising of the indigenous natural spirituality of humanity as it tried to break free of the corporate/religio-governmentally enforced repression.

Shamanism affords one the opportunity to experience these death and rebirth experiences as practice for conquering actual death, as well as to receive the indigenous teaching that can be passed on to those interested in doing the same. That this indigenous teaching recognizes the repression of the human soul, on a global level, should not be surprising. Each individual knows within themselves the natural path, and is wounded spiritually through past life experiences of repression. This is imbedded into the psyche, and manifests as a fear of those authority figures pushing this repression, or as a fear of challenging them. It is amazing the resistance an individual can muster in the reshaping of their belief system. Humans fiercely hold to their beliefs, rejecting anything that challenges their paradigm – even to the point of becoming themselves the enforcers of their own oppression. This is exactly that process which one goes through at death. The inability to let go of repressive belief is the conflict which forces death and rebirth, holding one within the revolving door of incarnation. The indigenous shamen, and writers of the Hindu Vedas, call this Samsara (the wheel of life).

So shamanism does operate on an individual basis. The teachings are in direct opposition to those societal, religious and political norms. The industrial revolution, high technology, and the established patriarchal systems of society have consciously attempted to stamp out the indigenous natural cultures of the planet under the guise of civilizing the savage man. I for one am not buying it. If there is to be some type of rebirth of the planet, global enlightenment, an entry into a golden age, it must be centered around the true nature of mankind, and not a rehashing of the same old fake status-quo. There will never be a global awakening which reveals that everything religion has taught us about sin, guilt, and repression of natural desires was right all along. The worse case scenario is if this oppressive religio-governmental society gains more and more control and ability to enforce their beliefs on more individuals. A literal hell-on-earth is the end result. It is up to us to rectify the situation When true indigenous spirituality cries from the deepest recesses of each of our souls, and the over-soul of humanity itself, to be set free, then we owe it to future generations not to let this happen to them.

The *Amanita muscaria* is the cornerstone of shamanism, producing the quintessential death and rebirth experience. Despite the fact that shamanism, by nature, rejects the yokes of patriarchal religion, shamanism is the cornerstone of all religions. Yet religion, as we have it today, by its very nature, has completely lost the natural indigenous freedom it professes to impart, the natural indigenous spiritual awakening for each individual by the plant of immortality, the most ancient of all spiritual traditions. In fact, it is the key to the individual's quest for immortality. This event is also the awakening of the spiritual being, which, although professed by most religious organizations, has an actuality that is seldom realized. Even shamanism, in its various forms, is certainly not without its patriarchal sub-groups, and sex-negative branches, all things can be polluted, and in this world it seems that anytime something good rises to the surface, the desire of man to gain control and power ends up ruining it. It is possible to cut through and discard these corruptions, and thus find a way to get at the real nature of what religion should be all about. There must be an underlying pattern discovered somewhere in the historical roots of human consciousness which gave birth to the common quest mythologies of the world. This puts forward a good case for mankind's indigenous, and most likely oldest, form of natural spirituality, shamanism.

Sexuality, Psychology, and the Big Picture

As I set out in this work to show the interconnectedness of the world's religions and also how they have fallen away from their seed resource (the *Amanita mus - caria*), I realized there is far too much to this subject to include in a single book. Also, I wanted to make the book short and to the point, so as not to drag the explanations out too much. In essence, the several religions mentioned are only a few of those connected. Because some were not mentioned by no means downplays their importance in history. There is much more to be written. So here in this last section I wish to touch upon a wide variety of subjects which are of importance to the overall view.

First off, let's cover the subject of psychology. Sigmund Freud was instrumental in the development of what can be considered the scientific understanding of human consciousness without the influence of religious dogma. Of course, we know that Freudian psychology has created an entire dogma of its own, but there is more to the story.

A newly released biography of Freud's life exposes the fact that Sigmund himself was an *Amanita* explorer. It details his hunting expeditions with his children through the forests gathering the mushrooms (*Amanita muscaria* in particular) for his experiments. As most people who have experienced different entheogens know, there is a profound look deep within the self that is associated with them, and whether you look at it as a psychological self-evaluation or a religious self-judgement process, the results are an intense self exploration. One's sexuality is often the central focus of this evaluation, and Freud was attempting to understand the human psyche in relation to this phenomenon. This is why the theories of Freud focus so much upon sexuality. Unfortunately, despite his attempts to figure this out in an unbiased way, his socially or religiously conditioned sex-negativity could not be set aside. He failed to recognize that sexually based trauma is dependant upon the sex-negative (patriarchically inspired) concepts that genital gratification is wrong and must be subdued. It is most often associated with childhood experiences, just as those memories that come to mind during the entheogenically expanded consciousness. It was the continuing research of his colleagues and students, Carl Jung and Wilhelm Reich, which identified the subjugation and repression of the sexual desires to be the culprit of neuroses, and not the gentility itself.

In essence, unless you believe that genital gratification is wrong, there is no trauma (except in the case of forced sexuality). This is of utmost importance to anyone who expands consciousness looking for answers. Guilt associated with sexuality can be a mind (and self) killer. This is why Reich wrote the book *The Invasion of Compulsory Sex Morality*. This and his many other books explains the error of Freud and others who continue to try to explain human psychology in sex-negative terms. He explains in *The Mass Psychology of Fascism* that the entire sex-negative and sex-oppressive philosophy is the basis of fascism. I have expressed throughout this work that the subjugation and control of others is largely caused by the seed of the omission of the mushroom in authorized religious dogma, but the subjugation and control of others is also the seed of the sex-negative concepts religious and societal dogma forces upon humanity. There is so much emphasis put upon sin as being a "universal law," that anyone who breaks these orders will be punished severely. It is fear imposed early in one's life that sex is bad, or must be authorized, that is often the source of sexual repression and the resultant debilitation of body and soul. This is as serious a problem as humanity can face.

Even though one finds that sex-negativity is an evil concept, rather than the great truth that it is purported to be, most every religion and modern society embraces the concept – so to openly discuss this rationally can draw the most rigorous of hostilities. If it were not so critical and important I would not find it necessary to bring it up, for fear of persecution myself. Wilhelm Reich was imprisoned by the U.S. federal government for writing about these things, then he mysteriously died in prison shortly after his incarceration. His books were confiscated by the government from the libraries and book stores all across the country - taken to New York - and burned in the incinerators. This happened in America, the supposed free speech herald of the world!

This understanding is extremely important; therefore I must risk my own safety in order to expose it. I do this for those of this generation and those that follow, or those that follow sometime in the future. It must be the eventual destiny of humanity to embrace the plant entheogens as spiritual tools and to be free to explore their individual sexual freedom if happiness, freedom, advancement, and truth are ever to be the basics of human existence, rather than oppression, subjugation, and sadness. Even John Allegro, author of *The Sacred Mushroom and the Cross,* took major hits for discussing sexuality and fertility cults and their importance in understanding the mushroom. He must have thought it was important or why face ridicule by including this aspect of religion in his work about mushrooms? According to Allegro, the sexuality of the early Christians (and their associated fertility rites) were kept secret and anything about it was written in code because of the heavy persecution from the Romans (or other sex-negative governments). Christianity has adopted the concept of the virgin birth, which simply takes away any sexuality from the birth of the god.

This is ridiculous for several reasons. There can be no birth without sex and the very word used to describe Mary (in the original Hebrew) was "Almah," which has no connection whatsoever with the word virgin. It means young woman. When this word was translated into Greek it was translated as "Parthenos," which does mean virgin. This is a drastic error, but it was fully an intentional one. How can sexuality be condemned when it was sex that created the god? Humanity is debilitated by sexual oppression and entheogenic prohibition whether it knows it or not. Anyone interested enough in spiritual plant entheogens to actually take the time to try them needs to understand this in order to rise above the dogma-associated guilt one can be consumed by if this is not made clear. What kind of teacher would I be if I were to withhold this crucial information?

Sometime in the future mankind will look back upon societies of the past as completely ridiculous in their attitudes and associated dogma, which were embraced (whether willingly or by force) in regards to plant entheogens and sexuality. But it will be understood that it was those who wished to exercise control and dominion over others that condemned these things (wrongly). While most people look at religious celebrities as holy and righteous, in awe of the wonderful cathedrals or beautiful garments they wear, or admire those who choose a life of celibacy (as in the case of priests or monks), I look at them as the promoters of evil and horrible lies, confusing the masses through false appearances. Is it any wonder that priests are getting in trouble for being sexual with the boys in their congregations? Is it a mystery that many monks are sexually active although it is forbidden? This happens because this celibacy idea is going against the very thing that gave them life itself, Mother Nature, this drives people to do all sorts of strange things. Reich also examined the fact that the suppression of natural sexual desires is the very thing that leads to perversions such as violent sexuality (rape), brutality, and sadism. It is the false sex-negative ideas that castrate man and genitally mutilate the women of the world in order to drive out the superimposed devil of sexual freedom; it's quite sickening.

Science has looked at the chimpanzee as our closest genetic relative, and to a certain extent modeled our society upon their Patriarchal system. Yet they are territorial; they fight and even murder one and other. The bonobo, another recently discovered primate, is Matriarchal, does not fight as the chimpanzee does, does not murder each other, and most importantly does have sexual contact freely with each other quite often. Is there something we can learn from this discovery? Firstly, the bonobo is genetically, DNA matched (percentage wise) closer to Homo sapien than the chimpanzee. Matriarchal societies and free-sex societies (Trobrianders for example) have been a part of human life in the past but have been systematically extinguished by the many Patriarchal systems alive and well today. Indoctrinated people feel compelled to save the heathen from their devilish ways and either force them to submit to their religion or annihilate them all together. Dancing naked on the full moon and open sexuality are part of some modern mystical traditions, which is one of the reasons they are associated with the devil and witchcraft, and condemned as evil by the self righteous. Those poor bastards! Will they never realize that they are keeping themselves down in the dire straits of despair and darkness by their own misguided beliefs? The judgement that they pass upon those free enough to express themselves and lucky enough to be associated with a sex-positive group of people is that same judgement which they will turn upon themselves in the end.

A knowledge that sexuality and genital gratification is of great value and must not be suppressed is what this is really all about. Witchcraft has also long been stereotyped as the little old lady living in the woods who has knowledge of herbs and has a cauldron for boiling up potions. A knowledge that the plants and herbs our planet has to offer are of great value is what this is really all about. Witchcraft and magick are condemned by many as evil and of the devil, yet those same people who think along those lines have no problem going to their shrink and gobbling down Prozac. So we must learn that the female should be exalted and worshipped, not crammed into a box of servitude to the misguided male influence. Sexual freedom and genital gratification are necessary for emotional stability and happiness. A full understanding of the plant kingdom is necessary to unlock the doorways of perception, making the pathway to enlightenment accessible. This is not new. Hundreds of thousands of people have read and understood Wilhelm Reich and see the fallacy of society and religion, and the ignorance of genital deprivation. Likewise, hundreds of thousands of people have read and understood the writings of Terence McKenna, John Allegro, Gordon Wasson, Clark Heinrich, Johnathan Ott, and others who have explained over and over again the implications of entheogenic plants as the seed source of religious experience. The question is, what will it take to get people to understand it, and do the things necessary to liberate themselves and the world?

Experiences of the Otherworldly Kind

Over the years I have had many meaningful experiences with the spiritual plant entheogen of my choice – the *Amanita muscaria*. Also, many of my friends, colleagues, and associates have journeyed there as well. I have been asked many times to give an example of some of the experiences that I have had. This is not as easy as it seems. The effect of time compression (thought processes are extremely fast) makes it difficult to describe the experience. Of course, since now is always now, the thing to comprehend is just how much is actually going on inside your head at that particular moment. While merging with the mushroom there is about a thousand times the normal amount of things usually going on, all at once. The experience of "seeing your life passing before your eyes" has been discussed previously, so here is one of the controlled events (meaning with a plan of action) which happened recently. I hope you can make some sense of it. Enjoy!

Friday, August 13th, 1999

The ideas of the cosmic influences of planetary alignments and lunar and solar eclipses led me to an understanding that there was, in our cosmology, a window of opportunity wherein those who happened to be aware of these events could effect a change on our planet for the better. With this in mind I began to put the pieces

The three candles to enlightenment.

together of how my understanding in my particular fields of research could be helpful in effecting this positive change through desire, motivation, and action. There is much research available right now dealing with these cosmic events. The lunar eclipse of July 28th, 1999; the solar eclipse of Aug 11th, 1999; and the Grand Cross alignment of planets in the fixed signs of the Zodiac on Aug 11th, 1999 (the fixed signs: Man,Bull, Eagle, Lion). The end (shift) date of August 13th, 1999, as the end (or major shift-point) of the Aztec Calendar (John Mini). The transference of Venus from the evening star to the Bright and Morning star during this same timeframe (natural cyclic process). The final phases of the shift (through the equinoctial procession) into the Age of Aquarius is 5/5/2000 (in the opinion of many). Without getting too much into the extrapolation and interpretation of these events, suffice it to say that there is theoretically pretty sound evidence that the events may be guiding us as a race into something extraordinary. Active and informed participation on an individual level seems to be tantamount to whether these events have an influence or not. Therefore I intended to do all I could, to the best of my abilities, to utilize my understanding in conjunction with others aware of these events, to plead the case to the powers that be of the loss of the freedoms and indigenous nature of mankind, and to voice a complaint regarding the oppression of those currently in the quest for truth, and those mutilated, tortured, imprisoned, and murdered through the Crusades, Inquisition, and ungodly laws of mankind over the past millennia.

The lunar eclipse of July 28th, 1999, was the first chapter in this current chain of amazing events, but had nearly escaped me. I had miscalculated it due to the time involved, and whereas I had intended to be well out of the city into my mountain retreat, I was caught by surprise and grounded deep in the big city. The event was nonetheless extraordinary. In my personal life I had just made reacquaintance with someone I deeply loved (C.P.) and then had lost contact with many years earlier. As the earth's shadow entered umbra (about 3:30 AM), I was suddenly swept away into a joyous and most profoundly expanded state of consciousness that seemed to psychically connect us in a sort of cosmic embrace that was spectacular. She was there with me, in my heart, and I felt completely entheogeically altered, yet was in no way so. In fact, it had been months since any such experiment had been attempted. The joy was indescribable, and like nothing I had ever before experienced. As I drifted off into sleep a few hours later, engulfed in the embrace of my lost love and "goddess," I realized a whole new understanding regarding the power and influence of astronomical events and their effects on consciousness and emotion.

The experiment went on as planned, although it was actually now a day after the eclipse. Upon awakening from a blissful sleep, I headed for the mountains.

The next few days were spent in a special mountain hideaway with a wonderful (and lovely) "procreative alchemist" and her sister (Karena and Jennifer). They were a joy and an inspiration as we discussed the upcoming (astronomical) events, and the particulars we could see played a major role in the shifting of the planetary consciousness. Hopefully to a world of freedom, without oppression. We could see how laws must be changed and how we might do our part in making these things possible. P.c. (Psilocybe) plant entheogens were used and inspired great states of awareness and insight into our own current states of knowing, as well as the current ongoing process of what can be affectionately called the evolutionary collective unconscious or the collective consciousness. The plants spoke to us.

We realized that evolution must happen in a leap, because otherwise the process to freedom and understanding was many years away. We could see a world where individuality and freedom were adored. We could see a world where people who developed great thoughts and understanding were rewarded much like a sports celebrity is today. We could visualize a world where plant spirits communicated with mankind, and research in this field attained university status. Experiments were important, and those who chose the field were regarded as brave and heroic. Levels of consciousness were quantifiable and measurable, and those who achieved high states were looked upon as teachers. We could visualize a world where human sexual desire was fulfilled, and as a result, perversions and rape were a thing of the past. Prohibition had ended, the black-market racketeers were forced to find legitimate businesses, the prisons were nearly emptied, theft was unnecessary, and police were truly there to help and serve. Is this not the Golden Age we are all hoping for? We were also profoundly aware of the current state, increasingly fascist police forces, black market drugs being networked by government officials (covertly controlling the gangs), truly addiction-breaking plants (Ibogaine) being made illegal and swept under the rug, childhood sexuality being forced into dark closets – amid threats not to tell – and secret societal ritual abuse.

The way we are going, there will be a camera in every home, on every street, in every bedroom. The military-like police will become completely uncontrollable and you will be unable to wake up in the morning without breaking some kind of law. Everyone will be on the government payroll (directly or in-directly), and all non state-authorized religious thought or comment will be a crime. This is where we are going without the intervention of truth. Our eventual destiny may be freedom and justice for all, but how long in the future will this be? How many people's lives must be destroyed before we realize what we truly need, and then desire it enough to actually make it happen? Success was achieved in this experiment. Our minds and hearts were opened, we could see things as they are, as they can and might become. It is, after all, up to all of us to become more aware.

The solar eclipse of August 11th, 1999, being connected symbolically to King Arthur and the quest for the Holy Grail, touching down at 11:11 in Cornwall England, was the second event for which I had a plan. The planets were moving into the Grand Cross alignment.

The Experiment Started on Wednesday, August 11th, 1999

I had just finished reading *Day of Destiny,* by John Mini, which calculates the shift-point or end of the Aztec calendar as being Friday, August 13th, 1999. This is an incredible book and I was very excited about doing an experiment on this date. The five plants were used as described in the cover artwork of this book. The *Amanita muscaria* was continually consumed and recycled starting on the 11th, for the full 3 days. Then the Syrian Rue (12th and 13th), then the P.c. (night of the 12th and through the 13th), and finally the Papaver was brewed for later (late on the 13th). Green herbs were used to quell the nausea. Throughout the night, visions were ecstatic, the plants were speaking, there were visions of timelessness. As the sun rose over the mountain to the east, I looked directly at it. Giant wings of light protruded from both sides and I saw the giant Aten (Egyptian winged disc) like I've never seen it before. All through the night, visions of possible futures were whirling through my thoughts. Fear of what the world might become, ecstasy at what it could become, and everything from joy at effecting change, to despair that all attempts to make the world a better place were futile.

There were six of us when we began this final evening and the experience became so intense that three had stumbled off to their tents to try to sleep. The three that were left were my friends Tom B., Sherry, and myself. We were the die-hards, and I had a mission. My idea was that something was going to make contact with our planet, after all, this was the shift-point. The normal things that I have grown familiar with (in the *Amanita* consciousness) were happening to us, such as a joining together of the minds. I felt the presence of billions of souls all hurtling through space in a sort of bubble, then it turned into a ship, a very, very large one. At one point I made the comment "Oh my god, that is a big ship" and Tom exclaimed "That's the first time I have ever had someone wake me out of a dream and describe exactly what I was dreaming." It is actually quite common on *Amanitas* for more than one person to see the exact same mental image. In fact, one time in about 1985 was the first time I found out about this A friend and I had consumed the *Amanitas* and after about 2 hours not much was happening. My friend decided to drive home (about 30 miles away). About a half hour after he left the mushrooms took effect in a big way. Suddenly, the visions I had included my friend – and the entire night we visualized the universe together. The next morning he called: "Man last night was a trip, huh?" My reply was, "What happened?"(not wanting to say anything first.) Then he said, "As I was pulling up to my house I started to see flashes, then I hurried in to lie down. I left my body and came to your place and was there all night." I was blown away. It was real! So I was pretty aware of the common consciousness phenomenon that Tom was experiencing for the first time.

So anyway, pardon my distraction. The sun was beaming lights that morning like a giant winged disc, and I knew this was the time I had prepared for. I prayed to the heavens. I called to the light, expressing through words and thoughts all that I knew about the sad state of affairs that I find the planet to be in. I called out that the indigenous nature of humanity had been oppressed, millions have been murdered, and there are dark forces controlling the governments and religions of the planet, please if anyone is listening; Help us! Just then I saw three lights circling the sun as they traveled across what looked like millions of miles towards me. As they approached I could feel their presence and feel their vibration. It was like nothing I have ever seen or felt before. They were literally humming at many harmonics, and at very high levels of frequency. They circled me. I looked at my compatriots who were unconscious. Then one of the lights broke from the circling and entered my body. I could feel the vibration. It was all so fast. My life was passing before my eyes.

The entity was literally becoming me in order to see who and what I was, and what I was all about. It saw everything. It knew me, it loved me, it saw my weaknesses and my human error, and it found me lacking. And I saw it too. Then it left, and the next of the three entered. Again becoming me, seeing me as all I am, I felt wonderful, it loved me, and I loved me, too. It showed me my faults, but showed me my strengths and good nature as well. I was in heaven! Then it left and the third one entered me. This was the most intense, exhaustive look into my deepest recesses. Emotions first were exalted, then sunk into despair as it showed me who I was by searching my memory and emotions. It was like a rollercoaster ride and I was soon exhausted. This last joining went on (although it is hard to gauge actual time) for about 20 minutes. Then it retreated. I once again saw the large boat of souls, and I was pulling the boat through space towards the sun. Then I broke away from the ship with what seemed to be a birthing process.

I exited the area of the sun and the ship, and was now outside of a huge bubble in space. Looking around, I could see there were billions of these bubbles. At the center of each bubble was a sun. Then I saw a giant dragon encapsulating the bubble I had just left. This dragon noticed me and I was then swept into a debate with it over the nature of humanity and all that it is. All I can say is that this great creature would make a point and I would argue the point, then another and another, it seemed to revolve around whether humanity should be enslaved and forced into submission by this great beast or not. I can't remember any particulars, although I have tried, but I do remember that I felt I had argued the case well (for whatever that is worth). I thought, "Is this what the mythological battling of the dragon is all about?" Well I can't really say, but I do know that I was sent back down into my body with a feeling of good and happiness (consumed the *Papaver*). I had done well. At least, if nothing else, I had made my point to whomever these entities in these visions were. I had achieved my goal. Something happened that day, exactly what, I don't really know for sure. Such is my life. I call for freedom of all mankind and hope that someone is listening. Until next time, fellow explorers of what we call life, I bid you farewell for now and may your life bring joy to you and the others that you touch.

There is much, much more to come.

James Arthur

DISCLAIMER

Statements found in this book are for informational purposes only. I am not suggesting or implying that anyone should consume anything, nor is the publisher. If you read this and decide to consume anything don't blame me (or the publisher) for your actions. Being a SHAMAN is not for the curious. It is a serious field of study with potentially dangerous substances involved. Like I said a million times, BE CAREFUL.

Recipe: Instructions and Cautions

As you may have heard, potency varies. The mushrooms picked early in the season seem to be a bit more potent than those at the end of the season. Although if you know exactly what this mushroom looks like, and I emphasize *exactly*, it is pretty difficult to mistake anything else for this very obvious mushroom. **Never eat ANY mushroom unless you are ABSOLUTELY 100% sure it is the one you want.** Many *Amanita* genus are deadly, as are many other species. This means BE VERY CAREFUL!!

I can not stress this enough. BE CAREFUL!! The author and publisher assume no responsibility for your actions.

This is some of the information that I feel is important for anyone that is interested in this experience. Since it is a "DEATH (and rebirth) EXPERIENCE" it is not for everyone. It bears NO resemblance to any other Entheogen (experience-wise) and this includes any other kind of mushroom.

Please take these precautions and suggestions very seriously.

One thing I need to mention right off the bat, is that most people throw up. So you would not want to do this alone as throwing up, while in any out of body experience, can be dangerous in itself. Many famous people have died from choking on their own vomit, do not make the same mistake.

Have friends (monitors) there for sure.

Make sure friends do not influence you in ANY way about your experience. No on site analysis.

Make sure friends know your hearing is intensified as well as your psychic perceptions, so NO conversations within your proximity, especially about your experience.

Have friends write down or record what you say.

Asking questions for clarity is ok, but avoid leading questions.

If you have a particular quest, write down your own questions for friends to ask you (as a reminder).

If 2 or more people do it together, they will often merge and have a communal experience. Like the Vulcan "mind meld."

Music does not matter once the state is achieved.

If you watch a movie you will BE the movie (so avoid boxing matches). This has been reported in the latter parts of stage 2 experience also. People who are familiar with shamanic/ecstatic trance will not be surprised if an explorer takes off all their clothes and runs around babbling. Know this is a possibility. Friends: If you have never seen first hand an initiation ecstatic-trance in South Africa or South America or at least a videotape of one, you may want to hunt some down. You will recognize it when you see it. Also, when someone enters the spirit realm they "put off" their bodies. This means they may hit the ground. Be prepared for this possi-

Freshly picked *Amanita muscaria*.

bility and prevent injuries accordingly. Write down what appears to be babbling because it will prove to be very unusual and interesting analysis material for later.

The Best Time and Place for *Amanitas*

Late night/early morning. Wide open spaces (no one in yelling range). The sunrise and sunlight are much better than the darkness, the light literally goes through you. You will feel yourself being born into light (feeling each and every cell as it changes). It is AWESOME!!!

A decent size cap is 6." Use 4 to 6, with stems (approximately 30 grams).

Dry them first (Decarboxylation), then crush or shred into powder or small pieces.

Add to 6 cups of water, keep just at boiling for 1 hour.

Strain and cool. Drink 1 to 1 1/2 cups. Or you can also just mix it relatively thin and drink the liquid with the pulp (this is what I suggest), but just consuming the strained material is easier (in case you are trying to keep this as easy as possible).

Wait 2 full hours for effects.

If desired effect is not achieved (you will definitely know) drink 1 more cup.

After 2 more hours, if the state is not achieved repeat.

Make sure you make water before your first cup, because the rest of your water you are going to re-ingest. Yes, I mean the consumption of your urine. It is merely an option, but highly recommended. Don't worry, it will not hurt you. In fact, if you're ill it will help your body fight off whatever ails you. Besides, you are a serious explorer aren't you? Remember, in the Christianity section I said that Jesus said to the woman at the well, "If you knew who I was, you would ask me for waters to drink." He was not kidding. It is an alchemical process even for those who are conditioned with repugnance to certain things. It is just an easier one to swallow if you are not fed a "proper" predisposition. Just chase it with some iced tea, you'll be fine. The post-alchemical-process material is much much better, and worth the effort. After first passing water wait an hour before consuming any more source material.

Hopefully you have had some practice with meditation. This comes into play because you are waking your spiritual consciousness into your surface consciousness state. There is also massive time compression.

Three States of Consciousness

This will help explain the experience:

1) Surface (conditioned) consciousness. Internal dialog and thought perception is approximately the same speed as voice (conversation).

2) Sub/supra (dream state) consciousness. Some time compression. Thought speed accelerated. Example: You may dream a whole day's event in a few minutes.

3) Spiritual (the real you) consciousness. Massive time compression. Thought speed accelerated massively. Possibly beyond time itself.

As in meditation you let all thoughts pass through you without reaction. You may experience a floating or sinking sensation. The Yogis say to go UP and hold yourself there. When you go "down" you experience the other side. If you go down you eventually will come back up. It seems the further down you go the higher you also go. This may seem confusing but while in the state you will understand.

The Three Stages of Effects:

1) The first stage is generally euphoric. Expect a lightness of being as well as an assumption of increased strength.

2) The second stage is where you will feel a lightness or a heaviness coming on. This is where you are starting to "put off" your physical body. Expect to feel like you are spiritually (and physically) falling through or shooting into space. You may feel an excessive HEAVINESS in your feet, legs (up to the knees or hips), then moving to the rest of your torso. If you lie down (highly recommended), you will feel your whole body getting heavy, and the sensation that you are flying out of it.

3) The third stage sometimes has an "in and out" effect as it comes on. You should definitely lie down when this happens. You will feel a FLASH that is a jump into another dimension. When this happens, if you are standing up you will fall down. So make sure you are lying comfortably as this starts to happen. These flashes will at first be instantaneous. Leaving and returning will allow glimpses of something completely different than your present surroundings. Then the flash turns into a full dimensional shift. This is when many people experience their life flashing before their eyes. You may start to panic, thinking you have eaten the wrong thing or have made a fatal mistake. This is where you will want your friends to reassure you that you are not going to die. Friends may also call the person by name and wake them temporarily. This is good for monitoring purposes because for the experiencer, things are happening so fast that there is no way to bring back all of the things that have been seen. If you do not reach the 3rd stage, you may want to try again at another time as THIS 3rd stage is where all the action is happening, and is the sought after effect.

Amanita muscaria is not similar to anything else. No other experiences have any relationship to this experience, except perhaps the traditional NDE (near death experience). When the time compression factor occurs, expect to see your life flashing before your eyes. The reason this is thought of as a near death experience is because of the NDE effect. If you understand the concept of reincarnation then you can grasp the concept that you have died before – maybe many, many times. Therefore this FLASH of your life before your eyes is familiar. This is not just a simple "hey, I felt like I was dying" thing. You LITERALLY KNOW you are dying because of the nature of the experience. If you are not familiar with (or a believer in) reincarnation, it has little bearing with the experience itself. Just know you will see your life flash before your eyes (interpret it as you will). I know that the whole extrapolation of this event is hard to believe, but if you feel inclined to do it by yourself (without friends) this is a choice I can only advise against. It's just a suggestion, but a VERY strong one.

INDEX

As A Bibliography (and reccommended reading list) I am listing authors by name rather than by works because each of the following authors should be read in their entirety.

Aaronson, Bernard
Acharya S
Albert Jr., David Bruce
Alford, Alan
Allegro, John Marco
Allen, John W.
Ananda (Aton and Odin
   Institute of Norway)
Arguelles, Jose
Arora, David
Awayan, Abd El Hakim
Barranger, Jack
Barrett, Francis
Bayley, Harold
Bennett, Chris
Blofeld, John
Boire, Richard Glen
Bonavia, E.
Bramley, William
Bryan, Karena
Budge, E. A. Wallace
Burgoyne, Thomas H.
Busenbark, Ernest
Callaway, Jace
Campbell, Joseph
Carpenter, Edward
Childress, David Hatcher
Clay, Albert T.
Davis, Wade
de Rios, Marlene Dobkin
Dekorne, Jim
Drury, Nevill
Dunn, Christopher
Eisenman, Robert
Eliade, Mircea
Escohotado, Antonio
Flattery, David S
Forte, Robert
Furst, Peter T.
Gardner, Laurence
Gartz, Jochen
Gèotz, Ignacio L.
Gimbutas, Maija
Govinda, Anagarika
Graves, Kersey
Graves, Robert
Grof, Stanislav
Gurdjieff, George Ivanovitch
Hall, Manley P.
Hapgood, Charles
Heinrich, Clark
Henry, William
Higgins, Godfrey
Hofmann, Albert
Holmstedt, Bo
Horn, Arthur and Lynette
Huxley, Aldous

Ingersoll, Ernest
Jung, Carl
Keith, Jim
King, L.W.
Leary, Timothy
Lewis, Spencer
Lilly, John
Luna, Luis Eduardo
Massey, Gerald
Mathers, S. Liddell MacGregor
Maxwell, Jordan
McKenna, Dennis
McKenna, Terance
Metzner, Ralph
Mini, John
Muller, Max
Mumford, John
O'Grady, Joan
Ott, Johnathan
Pinkham, Mark Amaru
Pye, Lloyd
Redfield, James
Regardie, Israel
Reich, Wilhelm
Robertson, J. M.
Ruck, Carl A. P.
Rudgley, Richard
Russell, Dan
Sandford, Jeremy
Sandison, R. A.
Schaefer, Stacy B.
Schonfield, Hugh J.
Schultes, Richard Evans
Schwartz, Martin
Sconfield, Hugh J.
Shulgin, Alexander (Sasha)
Sitchin, Zecharia
Smith, Houston
Spence, Lewis
St. Rain, Tédd
Stafford, Peter
Stamets, Paul
Streep, Peg
Temple, Robert
Tice, Paul
Titcomb, Sarah Elizabeth
Tompkins, Peter
Turner, D. M.
Valadez, Susana Eger
von Daniken, Erich
Walsh, Roger
Wasson, R. Gordon
Wells, Brian
Westropp, Hodder M.
Wilson, Colin
Wilson, Robert Anton

INDEX

Past Shock: The Origin of Religion and Its Impact on the Human Soul, by Jack Barranger. Twenty years ago, Alvin Toffler coined the term "future shock" — a syndrome in which people are overwhelmed by the future. *Past Shock* suggests that events that happened thousands of years ago very strongly impact humanity today. Technologically advanced beings created us as a slave race and in the process spiritually raped us. This book reveals the real reasons why religion was created, what organized religion won't tell you, the reality of the "slave chip" programming we all have to deal with, why we had to be created over and over again, what really happened in the Garden of Eden, what the Tower of Babel was and the reason why we were stopped from building it, how we were conditioned to remain spiritually ignorant, and much more. Jack exposes what he calls the "pretender gods," advanced beings who were not divine, but had advanced knowledge of scientific principles which included genetic engineering. Our advanced science of today has unraveled their secrets, and people like Barranger have the knowledge and courage to expose exactly how we were manipulated. Learn about our past conditioning, and how to overcome the "slave chip" mentality to begin living life as it was meant to be, as a spiritually fulfilled being. **ISBN 1-885395-08-6 • 126 pages • 6 x 9 • trade paper • illustrated • $12.95**

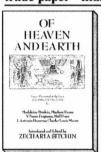

Of Heaven and Earth: Essays Presented at the First Sitchin Studies Day, edited by Zecharia Sitchin. Zecharia Sitchin's previous books have sold millions around the world. This book, first published in 1996, contains further information on his incredible theories about the origins of mankind and the intervention by intelligences beyond the Earth. Sitchin, in previous works, offers the most scholarly and convincing approach to the ancient astronaut theory you will most certainly ever find. This book offers the complete transcript of the first Sitchin Studies Day, held in Denver, Colorado on Oct. 6, 1996. Zecharia Sitchin's keynote address opens the book, followed by six other prominent speakers whose work has been influenced by Sitchin. The other contributors to the book include two university professors, a clergyman, a UFO expert, a philosopher, and a novelist—who joined Zecharia Sitchin in Denver, Colorado, to describe how his findings and conclusions have affected what they teach and preach. They all seem to agree that the myths of ancient peoples were actual events as opposed to being figments of imaginations. Another point of agreement is in Sitchin's work being the early part of a new paradigm—one that is already beginning to shake the very foundations of religion, archaeology and our society in general. **ISBN 1-885395-17-5 • 164 pages • 5 1/2 x 8 1/2 • trade paper • illustrated • $14.95**

Space Travelers and the Genesis of the Human Form: Evidence of Intelligent Contact in the Solar System, by Joan d'Arc. Believers in extraterrestrial intelligent life (ETI) have no doubt been confronted with the few standard arguments covered in this book that are pitched by most skeptics. But are they logical and internally consistent? Or are they based on mistaken assumptions, government-media hogwash, and outmoded scientific concepts? Even skeptics may want to explore the logical grounds upon which their staunch protest against the existence of ETI is founded. Can Darwinian evolution actually prove we are alone in the Universe? This book illustrates that Darwinian evolution is actually not an empirically predictable or testable scientific paradigm. Darwinian evolution is a circular argument which serves to keep Earth humans earthbound. The Space Travel Argument Against the Existence of ETI will be shown to be

dependent on three factors: (1) the persistent imposition of Earth-centered technological constraints (specifically, rocket technology and radio signals) implying an anthropocentric "you can't get here from there" attitude; (2) mathematical logic deduced from the faulty linear notions of Darwinian evolution, which only serve to put the "cart before the horse"; and (3) a circular and untestable hypothesis which essentially states "they aren't here because they aren't here." This book also shows that ancient anthropomorphic artifacts on Mars and the Moon are evidence of "Game Wardens" in our own solar system. Could the Earth be a controlled DNA repository for the ongoing creation and dissemination of life forms, including humans. **ISBN 1-58509-127-8 • 208 pages • 6 x 9 • trade paper • illustrated • $18.95**

100

Triumph of the Human Spirit: The Greatest Achievements of the Human Soul and How Its Power Can Change Your Life, by Paul Tice. A triumph of the human spirit happens when we know we are right about something, put our heart into achieving its goal, and then succeed. There is no better feeling. People throughout history have triumphed while fighting for the highest ideal of all -- spiritual truth. Tice brings you back to relive and explore history's most incredible spiritual moments, bringing you into the lives of visionaries and great leaders who were in touch with their souls and followed their hearts. They explored God in their own way, exposed corruption and false teachings, or freed themselves and others from suppression. People like Gandhi, Joan of Arc, and Dr. King expressed exactly what they believed and changed the entire course of history. They were eliminated through vio-

lence, but on a spiritual level achieved victory because of their strong moral cause. Their spirit lives on, and the world was greatly improved. Tice covers other movements and people who may have physically failed, but spiritually triumphed. This book not only documents the history of spiritual giants, it shows how you can achieve your own spiritual triumph. In today's world we are free to explore the truth without fear of being tortured or executed. As a result, the rewards are great. Various exercises will strengthen the soul and reveal its hidden power. One can discover their true spiritual source with this work and will be able to tap into it. This is the perfect book for all those who believe in spiritual freedom and have a passion for the truth. **ISBN 1-885395-57-4 · 295 pages · 6 x 9 · trade paper · illustrated · $19.95**

That Old Time Religion: The Story of Religious Foundations, by **Jordan Maxwell and Paul Tice.** This book proves there is nothing new under the sun regarding many of our modern religious beliefs. This includes Christianity, and how many of its beliefs could be far older than what we have suspected. It gives a complete run-down of the stellar, lunar, and solar evolution of our religious systems and contains new, long-awaited, exhaustive research on the gods and our beliefs. The book's central theme, the origin of religions, centers around the work of Jordan Maxwell. Mr. Maxwell has become widely known as one of the world's foremost experts on early mythological systems and their influence on both ancient and modern religions. He continually surprises the reader with factual evidence on where our modern beliefs *really* came from. The book also includes an interview with Dr. Alan A. Snow, famous Dead Sea Scrolls scholar, on astrology in the Dead Sea Scrolls. Dr. Snow has been referred to by Sydney Ohmarr as the "world's greatest authority on astrology and the Dead Sea Scrolls." Three chapters are also included by Paul Tice, a teacher of Gnostic principles. He adds a more spiritual dimension to our current belief structures in the last chapter, explaining how we should revert to the original teachings of Jesus, and others. This would allow us to understand their teachings before they had become corrupted by "organized religion." This book is illustrated, organized, and very comprehensible. Educate yourself with clear documented proof, and be prepared to have your belief system shattered! **ISBN 1-58509-100-6 · 103 pages · 6 x 9 · trade paper · $12.95**

Mysteries Explored: The Search for Human Origins, UFOs, and Religious Beginnings, by **Jack Barranger and Paul Tice**. Jack Barranger and Paul Tice are two authors who have combined forces in an overall investigation into human origins, religion, mythology, UFOs, and other unexplained phenomena. In the first chapter, "The Legacy of Zecharia Sitchin", Barranger covers the importance of Sitchin's *Earth Chronicles* books, which is creating a revolution in the way we look at our past. In "The First Dragon" chapter, Tice examines the earliest known story containing dragons, coming from Sumerian/Babylonian mythology.

In "Past Shock", Barranger suggests that events which happened thousands of years ago very strongly impact humanity today. In "UFOs: From Earth or Outer Space?" Tice explores the evidence for aliens being from other earthly dimensions as opposed to having an extraterrestrial origin. "Is Religion Harmful?" looks at the origins of religion and why the entire idea may no longer be working for us, while "A Call to Heresy" shows how Jesus and the Buddha were considered heretics in their day, and how we have reached a critical point in our present spiritual development that requires another such leap. Aside from these chapters, the book also contains a number of outrageous (but discontinued) newsletters, including: Promethean Fire, Pleiadian Poop, and Intrusions. **ISBN 1-58509-101-4 · 103 pages · 6 x 9 · trade paper · $12.95**

Of Heaven and Earth: Essays Presented at the First Sitchin Studies Day, edited by Zecharia Sitchin. ISBN 1-885395-17-5 • 164 pages • 5 1/2 x 8 1/2 • trade paper • illustrated • $14.95

God Games: What Do You Do Forever?, by Neil Freer. ISBN 1-885395-39-6 • 312 pages • 6 x 9 • trade paper • $19.95

Space Travelers and the Genesis of the Human Form: Evidence of Intelligent Contact in the Solar System, by Joan d'Arc. ISBN 1-58509-127-8 • 208 pages • 6 x 9 • trade paper • illustrated • $18.95

Humanity's Extraterrestrial Origins: ET Influences on Humankind's Biological and Cultural Evolution, by Dr. Arthur David Horn with Lynette Mallory-Horn. ISBN 3-931652-31-9 • 373 pages • 6 x 9 • trade paper • $17.00

Past Shock: The Origin of Religion and Its Impact on the Human Soul, by Jack Barranger. ISBN 1-885395-08-6 • 126 pages • 6 x 9 • trade paper • illustrated • $12.95

Flying Serpents and Dragons: The Story of Mankind's Reptilian Past, by R.A. Boulay. ISBN 1-885395-38-8 • 276 pages • 6 x 9 • trade paper • illustrated • $19.95

Triumph of the Human Spirit: The Greatest Achievements of the Human Soul and How Its Power Can Change Your Life, by Paul Tice. ISBN 1-885395-57-4 • 295 pages • 6 x 9 • trade paper • illustrated • $19.95

Mysteries Explored: The Search for Human Origins, UFOs, and Religious Beginnings, by Jack Barranger and Paul Tice. ISBN 1-58509-101-4 • 104 pages • 6 x 9 • trade paper • $12.95

Mushrooms and Mankind: The Impact of Mushrooms on Human Consciousness and Religion, by James Arthur. ISBN 1-58509-151-0 • 103 pages • 6 x 9 • trade paper • $12.95

Vril or Vital Magnetism, with an Introduction by Paul Tice. ISBN 1-58509-030-1 • 124 pages • 5 1/2 x 8 1/2 • trade paper • $12.95

The Odic Force: Letters on Od and Magnetism, by Karl von Reichenbach. ISBN 1-58509-001-8 • 192 pages • 6 x 9 • trade paper • $15.95

The New Revelation: The Coming of a New Spiritual Paradigm, by Arthur Conan Doyle. ISBN 1-58509-220-7 • 124 pages • 6 x 9 • trade paper • $12.95

The Astral World: Its Scenes, Dwellers, and Phenomena, by Swami Panchadasi. ISBN 1-58509-071-9 • 104 pages • 6 x 9 • trade paper • $11.95

Reason and Belief: The Impact of Scientific Discovery on Religious and Spiritual Faith, by Sir Oliver Lodge. ISBN 1-58509-226-6 • 180 pages • 6 x 9 • trade paper • $17.95

William Blake: A Biography, by Basil De Selincourt. ISBN 1-58509-225-8 • 384 pages • 6 x 9 • trade paper • $28.95

The Divine Pymander: And Other Writings of Hermes Trismegistus, translated by John D. Chambers. ISBN 1-58509-046-8 • 196 pages • 6 x 9 • trade paper • $16.95

Theosophy and The Secret Doctrine, by Harriet L. Henderson. Includes **H.P. Blavatsky: An Outline of Her Life,** by Herbert Whyte, ISBN 1-58509-075-1 • 132 pages • 6 x 9 • trade paper • $13.95

The Light of Egypt, Volume One: The Science of the Soul and the Stars, by Thomas H. Burgoyne. ISBN 1-58509-051-4 • 320 pages • 6 x 9 • trade paper • illustrated • $24.95

The Light of Egypt, Volume Two: The Science of the Soul and the Stars, by Thomas H. Burgoyne. ISBN 1-58509-052-2 • 224 pages • 6 x 9 • trade paper • illustrated • $17.95

The Jumping Frog and 18 Other Stories: 19 Unforgettable Mark Twain Stories, by Mark Twain. ISBN 1-58509-200-2 • 128 pages • 6 x 9 • trade paper • $12.95

The Devil's Dictionary: A Guidebook for Cynics, by Ambrose Bierce. ISBN 1-58509-016-6 • 144 pages • 6 x 9 • trade paper • $12.95

The Smoky God: Or The Voyage to the Inner World, by Willis George Emerson. ISBN 1-58509-067-0 • 184 pages • 6 x 9 • trade paper • illustrated • $15.95

A Short History of the World, by H.G. Wells. ISBN 1-58509-211-8 • 320 pages • 6 x 9 • trade paper • $24.95

The Voyages and Discoveries of the Companions of Columbus, by Washington Irving. ISBN 1-58509-500-1 • 352 pages • 6 x 9 • hard cover • $39.95

History of Baalbek, by Michel Alouf. ISBN 1-58509-063-8 • 196 pages • 5 x 8 • trade paper • illustrated • $15.95

Ancient Egyptian Masonry: The Building Craft, by Sommers Clarke and R. Engelback. ISBN 1-58509-059-X • 350 pages • 6 x 9 • trade paper • illustrated • $26.95

That Old Time Religion: The Story of Religious Foundations, by Jordan Maxwell and Paul Tice. ISBN 1-58509-100-6 • 103 pages • 6 x 9 • trade paper • $12.95

Jumpin' Jehovah: Exposing the Atrocities of the Old Testament God, by Paul Tice. ISBN 1-58509-102-2 • 104 pages • 6 x 9 • trade paper • $12.95

The Book of Enoch: A Work of Visionary Revelation and Prophecy, Revealing Divine Secrets and Fantastic Information about Creation, Salvation, Heaven and Hell, translated by R. H. Charles. ISBN 1-58509-019-0 • 152 pages • 5 1/2 x 8 1/2 • trade paper • $13.95

The Book of Enoch: Translated from the Editor's Ethiopic Text and Edited with an Enlarged Introduction, Notes and Indexes, Together with a Reprint of the Greek Fragments, edited by R. H. Charles. ISBN 1-58509-080-8 • 448 pages • 6 x 9 • trade paper • $34.95

The Book of the Secrets of Enoch, translated from the Slavonic by W. R. Morfill. Edited, with Introduction and Notes by R. H. Charles. ISBN 1-58509-020-4 • 148 pages • 5 1/2 x 8 1/2 • trade paper • $13.95

Enuma Elish: The Seven Tablets of Creation, Volume One, by L. W. King. ISBN 1-58509-041-7 • 236 pages • 6 x 9 • trade paper • illustrated • $18.95

Enuma Elish: The Seven Tablets of Creation, Volume Two, by L. W. King. ISBN 1-58509-042-5 • 260 pages • 6 x 9 • trade paper • illustrated • $19.95

Enuma Elish, Volumes One and Two: The Seven Tablets of Creation, by L. W. King. Two volumes from above bound as one. ISBN 1-58509-043-3 • 496 pages • 6 x 9 • trade paper • illustrated • $38.90

The Archko Volume: Documents that Claim Proof to the Life, Death, and Resurrection of Christ, by Drs. McIntosh and Twyman. ISBN 1-58509-082-4 • 248 pages • 6 x 9 • trade paper • $20.95

The Lost Language of Symbolism: An Inquiry into the Origin of Certain Letters, Words, Names, Fairy-Tales, Folklore, and Mythologies, by Harold Bayley. ISBN 1-58509-070-0 • 384 pages • 6 x 9 • trade paper • $27.95

The Book of Jasher: A Suppressed Book that was Removed from the Bible, Referred to in Joshua and Second Samuel, translated by Albinus Alcuin (800 AD). ISBN 1-58509-081-6 • 304 pages • 6 x 9 • trade paper • $24.95

The Bible's Most Embarrassing Moments, with an Introduction by Paul Tice. ISBN 1-58509-025-5 • 172 pages • 5 x 8 • trade paper • $14.95

History of the Cross: The Pagan Origin and Idolatrous Adoption and Worship of the Image, by Henry Dana Ward. ISBN 1-58509-056-5 • 104 pages • 6 x 9 • trade paper • illustrated • $11.95

Was Jesus Influenced by Buddhism? A Comparative Study of the Lives and Thoughts of Gautama and Jesus, by Dwight Goddard. ISBN 1-58509-027-1 • 252 pages • 6 x 9 • trade paper • $19.95

History of the Christian Religion to the Year Two Hundred, by Charles B. Waite. ISBN 1-885395-15-9 • 556 pages. • 6 x 9 • hard cover • $25.00

Symbols, Sex, and the Stars, by Ernest Busenbark.ISBN 1-885395-19-1 • 396 pages • 5 1/2 x 8 1/2 • trade paper • $22.95

History of the First Council of Nice: A World's Christian Convention, A.D. 325, by Dean Dudley. ISBN 1-58509-023-9 • 132 pages • 5 1/2 x 8 1/2 • trade paper • $12.95

The World's Sixteen Crucified Saviors, by Kersey Graves. ISBN 1-58509-018-2 • 436 pages • 5 1/2 x 8 1/2 • trade paper • $29.95

Babylonian Influence on the Bible and Popular Beliefs: A Comparative Study of Genesis I.2, by A. Smythe Palmer. ISBN 1-58509-000-X • 124 pages • 6 x 9 • trade paper • $12.95

Biography of Satan: Exposing the Origins of the Devil, by Kersey Graves. ISBN 1-885395-11-6 • 168 pages • 5 1/2 x 8 1/2 • trade paper • $13.95

The Malleus Maleficarum: The Notorious Handbook Once Used to Condemn and Punish "Witches," by Heinrich Kramer and James Sprenger. ISBN 1-58509-098-0 • 332 pages • 6 x 9 • trade paper • $25.95

Crux Ansata: An Indictment of the Roman Catholic Church, by H. G. Wells. ISBN 1-58509-210-X • 160 pages • 6 x 9 • trade paper • $14.95

Emanuel Swedenborg: The Spiritual Columbus, by U.S.E. (William Spear). ISBN 1-58509-096-4 • 208 pages • 6 x 9 • trade paper • $17.95

Dragons and Dragon Lore, by Ernest Ingersoll. ISBN 1-58509-021-2 • 228 pages • 6 x 9 • trade paper • illustrated • $17.95

The Vision of God, by Nicholas of Cusa. ISBN 1-58509-004-2 • 160 pages • 5 x 8 • trade paper • $13.95

The Historical Jesus and the Mythical Christ: Separating Fact From Fiction, by Gerald Massey. ISBN 1-58509-073-5 • 244 pages • 6 x 9 • trade paper • $18.95

Gog and Magog: The Giants in Guildhall; Their Real and Legendary History, with an Account of Other Giants at Home and Abroad, by F.W. Fairholt. ISBN 1-58509-084-0 • 172 pages • 6 x 9 • trade paper • $16.95

The Origin and Evolution of Religion, by Albert Churchward. ISBN 1-58509-078-6 • 504 pages • 6 x 9 • trade paper • $39.95

The Origin of Biblical Traditions, by Albert T. Clay. ISBN 1-58509-065-4 • 220 pages • 5 1/2 x 8 1/2 • trade paper • $17.95

Aryan Sun Myths, by Sarah Elizabeth Titcomb, Introduction by Charles Morris. ISBN 1-58509-069-7 • 192 pages • 6 x 9 • trade paper • $15.95

The Social Record of Christianity, by Joseph McCabe. Includes *The Lies and Fallacies of the Encyclopedia Britannica,* ISBN 1-58509-215-0 • 204 pages • 6 x 9 • trade paper • $17.95

The History of the Christian Religion and Church During the First Three Centuries, by Dr. Augustus Neander. ISBN 1-58509-077-8 • 112 pages • 6 x 9 • trade paper • $12.95

Ancient Symbol Worship: Influence of the Phallic Idea in the Religions of Antiquity, by Hodder M. Westropp and C. Staniland Wake. ISBN 1-58509-048-4 • 120 pages • 6 x 9 • trade paper • illustrated • $12.95

The Gnosis: Or Ancient Wisdom in the Christian Scriptures, by William Kingsland. ISBN 1-58509-047-6 • 232 pages • 6 x 9 • trade paper • $18.95

The Evolution of the Idea of God: An Inquiry into the Origin of Religions, by Grant Allen. ISBN 1-58509-074-3 • 160 pages • 6 x 9 • trade paper • $14.95

Sun Lore of All Ages: A Survey of Solar Mythology, Folklore, Customs, Worship, Festivals, and Superstition, by William Tyler Olcott. ISBN 1-58509-044-1 • 316 pages • 6 x 9 • trade paper • $24.95

Nature Worship: An Account of Phallic Faiths and Practices Ancient and Modern, by the Author of Phallicism with an Introduction by Tedd St. Rain.ISBN 1-58509-049-2 • 112 pages • 6 x 9 • trade paper • illustrated • $12.95

Life and Religion, by Max Muller. ISBN 1-885395-10-8 • 237 pages • 5 1/2 x 8 1/2 • trade paper • $14.95

Jesus: God, Man, or Myth? An Examination of the Evidence, by Herbert Cutner. ISBN 1-58509-072-7 • 304 pages • 6 x 9 • trade paper • $23.95

Pagan and Christian Creeds: Their Origin and Meaning, by Edward Carpenter. ISBN 1-58509-024-7 • 316 pages • 5 1/2 x 8 1/2 • trade paper • $24.95

The Christ Myth: A Study, by Elizabeth Evans. ISBN 1-58509-037-9 • 136 pages • 6 x 9 • trade paper • $13.95

Popery: Foe of the Church and the Republic, by Joseph F. Van Dyke. ISBN 1-58509-058-1 • 336 pages • 6 x 9 • trade paper • illustrated • $25.95

Career of Religious Ideas, by Hudson Tuttle. ISBN 1-58509-066-2 • 172 pages • 5 x 8 • trade paper • $15.95

Buddhist Suttas: Major Scriptural Writings from Early Buddhism, by T.W. Rhys Davids.ISBN 1-58509-079-4 • 376 pages • 6 x 9 • trade paper • $27.95

Early Buddhism, by T. W. Rhys Davids. Includes **Buddhist Ethics: The Way to Salvation?,** by Paul Tice. ISBN 1-58509-076-X • 112 pages • 6 x 9 • trade paper • $12.95

The Fountain-Head of Religion: A Comparative Study of the Principal Religions of the World and a Manifestation of their Common Origin from the Vedas, by Ganga Prasad. ISBN 1-58509-054-9 • 276 pages • 6 x 9 • trade paper • $22.95

India: What Can It Teach Us?, by Max Muller. ISBN 1-58509-064-6 • 284 pages • 5 1/2 x 8 1/2 • trade paper • $22.95

Matrix of Power: How the World has Been Controlled by Powerful People Without Your Knowledge, by Jordan Maxwell. ISBN 1-58509-120-0 • 104 pages • 6 x 9 • trade paper • $12.95

Cyberculture Counterconspiracy: A Steamshovel Web Reader, Volume One, edited by Kenn Thomas. ISBN 1-58509-125-1 • 180 pages • 6 x 9 • trade paper • illustrated • $16.95

Cyberculture Counterconspiracy: A Steamshovel Web Reader, Volume Two, edited by Kenn Thomas. ISBN 1-58509-126-X • 132 pages • 6 x 9 • trade paper • illustrated • $13.95

Oklahoma City Bombing: The Suppressed Truth, by Jon Rappoport. ISBN 1-885395-22-1 • 112 pages • 5 1/2 x 8 1/2 • trade paper • $12.95

The Protocols of the Learned Elders of Zion, by Victor Marsden. ISBN 1-58509-015-8 • 312 pages • 6 x 9 • trade paper • $24.95

Secret Societies and Subversive Movements, by Nesta H. Webster. ISBN 1-58509-092-1 • 432 pages • 6 x 9 • trade paper • $29.95

The Secret Doctrine of the Rosicrucians, by Magus Incognito. ISBN 1-58509-091-3 • 256 pages • 6 x 9 • trade paper • $20.95

The Origin and Evolution of Freemasonry: Connected with the Origin and Evolution of the Human Race, by Albert Churchward.ISBN 1-58509-029-8 • 240 pages • 6 x 9 • trade paper • $18.95

The Lost Key: An Explanation and Application of Masonic Symbols, by Prentiss Tucker. ISBN 1-58509-050-6 • 192 pages • 6 x 9 • trade paper • illustrated • $15.95

The Character, Claims, and Practical Workings of Freemasonry, by Rev. C.G. Finney. ISBN 1-58509-094-8 • 288 pages • 6 x 9 • trade paper • $22.95

The Secret World Government or "The Hidden Hand": The Unrevealed in History, by Maj.-Gen., Count Cherep-Spiridovich. ISBN 1-58509-093-X • 203 pages • 6 x 9 • trade paper • $17.95

The Magus, Book One: A Complete System of Occult Philosophy, by Francis Barrett. ISBN 1-58509-031-X • 200 pages • 6 x 9 • trade paper • illustrated • $16.95

The Magus, Book Two: A Complete System of Occult Philosophy, by Francis Barrett. ISBN 1-58509-032-8 • 220 pages • 6 x 9 • trade paper • illustrated • $17.95

The Magus, Book One and Two: A Complete System of Occult Philosophy, by Francis Barrett. ISBN 1-58509-033-6 • 420 pages • 6 x 9 • trade paper • illustrated • $34.90

The Key of Solomon The King, by S. Liddell MacGregor Mathers. ISBN 1-58509-022-0 • 152 pages • 6 x 9 • trade paper • illustrated • $12.95

Magic and Mystery in Tibet, by Alexandra David-Neel. ISBN 1-58509-097-2 • 352 pages • 6 x 9 • trade paper • $26.95

The Comte de St. Germain, by I. Cooper Oakley. ISBN 1-58509-068-9 • 280 pages • 6 x 9 • trade paper • illustrated • $22.95

Alchemy Rediscovered and Restored, by A. Cockren. ISBN 1-58509-028-X • 156 pages • 5 1/2 x 8 1/2 • trade paper • $13.95

The 6th and 7th Books of Moses, with an Introduction by Paul Tice. ISBN 1-58509-045-X • 188 pages • 6 x 9 • trade paper • illustrated • $16.95

Printed in the United States
22329LVS00006BA/19-33

9 781585 091515